MW00576291

The Psychology of Tzimtzum

Self, Other, and God

מגיד

MAGGID

Mordechai Rotenberg

THE PSYCHOLOGY

OF TZIMTZUM

SELF

OTHER

AND

GOD

Maggid Books

The Psychology of Tzimtzum
Self, Other, and God

First English Edition, 2015

Maggid Books
An imprint of Koren Publishers Jerusalem Ltd.

POB 8531, New Milford, CT 06776-8531, USA
& POB 4044, Jerusalem 9104001, Israel
www.korenpub.com

Original Hebrew Edition © Mordechai Rotenberg, 2010
English Translation © Koren Publishers Jerusalem Ltd., 2015

The publication of this book was made possible
through the generous support of *Torah Education in Israel*.

ISBN 978-1-59264-384-4, *hardcover*

A CIP catalogue record for this title is
available from the British Library

Printed and bound in the United States

In memory of my dear friend,
Naphtali Lau-Lavie,
personifier of Shoah and rebirth.

The translation of this book was partially sponsored by
the Robert Freund Foundation,
which has been actively involved in the publication
and dissemination of Mordechai Rotenberg's books.

Contents

Preface

For many years during my academic career, I would write about anything. I wrote out of insecurity: I constantly dreaded the wrath of some hypothetical harsh critic. As I wrote at eye level – or, more precisely, cross-eyed level – with my readers, I was in continual fear of some potential faultfinder in any of the fields I touched on. Frankly, my touch was very slight, if not too slight; it was the touch of an outsider, of someone who did not quite feel at home in any field. Today, I write in order to reach my readers – whoever they might be – and to look them straight in the eye, and I try to write for all those who wish to read what I have to say.

Over the years, I have developed a psychology of Tzimtzum (self-contraction, as I explain below) inspired by kabbalistic Hasidism, which I am presenting in this book as an introduction to my readers. They were also years of an ongoing struggle for recognition of ideas that raised a few eyebrows but which gradually earned considerable esteem. Today, the psychology of Tzimtzum enjoys greater recognition and is steadily growing. This preface is an opportunity to describe the process I underwent in order to develop these ideas.

In the 1960s, I was a parole officer for juvenile offenders and acquired considerable experience working with distressed youth. I decided to do a master's degree at New York University and during my studies there, in 1962, a Jewish professor of anthropology told me he would like to make a proposition. He had heard through the grapevine about a Jewish student who was doing a degree in criminology and who was a descendant of the first Gerer Rebbe and founder of the Ger hasidic sect, Rabbi Yitzhak Meir Alter. This professor wanted me to write a doctorate under his guidance on the psychology of Hasidism. I politely but firmly turned down his offer. Precisely because I was a scion of a many-branched hasidic family, I rejected the idea: I was afraid of my family's reaction after learning that I was using Hasidism's sacred traditions in the non-Jewish world of the university. I was simply not interested in such a project.

I continued my studies at Berkeley, in the latter half of the 1960s. Even in those days, Berkeley was considered the most strongly leftist Ivy League college campus and the late 1960s was its golden era. During that period, everyone at Berkeley was against something: the education system; the Vietnam War; even in my own discipline, the opponents of psychiatry belonged to what they called the anti-psychiatric movement. The arguments against psychiatry primarily focused on psychiatric diagnosis as a mark of Cain. In other fields of medicine, if no evidence of a physical illness can be found, a physician must conclude the report of a physical examination with the acronym NPF (no pathological findings), signifying that the patient is healthy. In contrast, in psychiatry, there is no such diagnosis as NPF.

I began to investigate why NPF was not a term used in psychiatry. It was clear to me that the roots of psychiatric labels were not to be found in psychiatry itself. I discovered that, in the past, insane individuals were defined in a very different manner. There were periods when they were described as being possessed by the Devil. Despite the frightening image of such demonology, I detected its optimistic message: insane individuals were essentially healthy people who were possessed by the Devil but who could be liberated from that condition, whereupon they would again be considered perfectly healthy. So from where, I asked myself, came the belief that the mentally ill were incurable?

During that period, I immersed myself in the writings of the classic sociologist Max Weber, who frequently refers to the religious roots of secular culture. His most famous argument concerns the Protestant-Calvinistic roots of capitalism, namely, that the drive for economic success is derived from Calvinism's deterministic theory, by which the religious worth of all individuals is divinely predetermined and the only way for an individual to prove that he or she is indeed one of God's chosen is to attain material success in this world.

What caught my eye in this sociological depiction of Protestantism was not the situation of those who are described as the "chosen ones," but rather those who were considered to be cursed. Although based on a model similar to Weber's, my argument focused not on the achievers but on the "losers": just as economics allows society to identify the achievers, psychiatry enables it to define the "cursed ones." The Protestant ethic, I argued, created the idea that mental illness was incurable.

I began to speak about my theory, and I quickly found myself at the center of a controversy. I was invited to speak at international conferences in both the western and eastern hemispheres, where my ideas were introduced and debated. I started to realize that, in the academic world of which I was both a member and a captive, I had to state clearly that I was the founder of this thesis and publicize it widely. I wrote an article that expanded into a book, *Damnation and Deviance: The Protestant Ethic and the Spirit of Failure* (Free Press, 1978), which created quite a stir.

In that book, after analyzing historical findings regarding devout Christian societies, the process of psychiatric labeling, and the connection between those societies and this process, I wrote an upbeat chapter about the possibility of another kind of psychiatry, one that was based on the approach of the Baal Shem Tov, the founder of Hasidism, and which offered the option of an optimistic psychology more interested in the future than in the past. This chapter drew considerable attention from the publishers, who began to ask me many questions about Hasidism. They were very interested in it and did not know the difference between Hasidism as a religious movement and Hasidism as a general expression of religious devotion. Inspired by their curiosity, I became curious myself.

I was on sabbatical, and, because of family circumstances, I frequently traveled by train. During those long journeys, I spent time considering whether there was such a thing as hasidic psychology and, if it did exist, whether it could contribute to the more familiar brand of psychology. On one of those train rides, I thought about the idea of Tzimtzum. I became very excited and the train I was traveling on suddenly became a heavenly chariot. After I got off the train, I felt as if I were floating to my university department. I began writing and, after twenty minutes, I produced the outline of what would later become a book on existence based on the secret of Tzimtzum.

According to the kabbalistic notion of Tzimtzum, God contracts Himself in order to make room for the human world. I realized that the concept had immense psychological and educational potential. For human beings seeking to emulate God, it could serve as a model to make room for others with whom they seek to develop a dialogic relationship.

And yet, I must admit, I was hesitant. All I knew about Hasidism was what my father had taught me. I had no scholarly background in my understanding of Hasidism. How could I say anything meaningful in the presence of such great scholars of Jewish mysticism as Martin Buber and Gershom Scholem without embarrassing myself? The late Professor Yisrael Moshe Ta-Shma arranged a meeting for me with Professor Moshe Idel, who encouraged me to pursue my thinking with regard to Tzimtzum. Idel told me that Tzimtzum was a central concept both in Kabbala and Hasidism; that it was a uniquely Jewish idea. (During the *shiva* period of mourning following Ta-Shma's death, his widow commented that he would often say he had been brought to this world specifically for the purpose of introducing me to Idel.) Idel, who later became a leading scholar of Kabbala, tried to get me involved in research on the texts themselves that deal with Tzimtzum. However, I insisted on leaving the textual research to scholars like him; I wanted to focus instead on the study of the possible contribution of hasidic and kabbalistic texts to the psychology of daily life.

I wrote a number of additional books, sharpening my focus on the psychology of Tzimtzum, which had become a basic paradigm in my thinking. The idea that two opposing elements could face each other and actually promote, rather than diminish, each other, became a very fertile ground. I began to think about mutually productive pairs: man and woman, impulse (*yetzer*) and creativity (*yetzira*), temple (*mikdash*) and midrash, life and death. Professor Yehuda Liebes taught me about the centrality of this model of pairing in Kabbala: the two elements in the pair must be merged and their connection transformed from contradictory to harmonious, filling the world with life through letter rearrangement: *nittuk* (N-T-K, disconnection) becomes *tikkun* (T-K-N, amendment) and *ayin* or *ein* (A-Y-N, nothingness) becomes *ani* (A-N-Y, I or ego).

Over the years, the concept of Tzimtzum has attracted students such as Dr. Baruch Kahana and my daughter, Dr. Michal Fachler, who were prepared to devote themselves to exploring it further. Together with these students, I began to accumulate considerable clinical experience. In 2006, my wife Naomi and I founded the Center for Jewish Psychology, in memory of our son, Boaz, who fell in the early days of the First Intifada while serving in an elite special-operations paratroopers unit in the Israel Defense Forces. The Center gradually grew, and with it the interest in, and professional recognition of, the Jewish psychology of Tzimtzum. In 2009, I was awarded the Israel Prize for Social Work. This prize means a great deal to me, after so many years of writing against conventional thinking.

When the original Hebrew book appeared, I felt that I had to apologize to my readers for the title *Introduction to the Psychology of Tzimtzum*, which uses a Greek term, *psychology*, rather than a Hebrew one. However, the word *psychology* contains both the concept of mental health care and the specific socio-cultural context that my book is aimed at. The repeated references to psychoanalysis are not intended to reflect a "forced return" to Freud. However, I do wish to refer to Freud's Oedipal individual as a symbol of a broad cultural heritage that goes well beyond the confines of clinical psychology.

Through the thirteen books I have written in the course of over forty years of academic work, I have developed a theory of Jewish psychology derived from the tradition of Jewish exegesis that relates to the different dimensions of each individual's activities and life. While recent rabbinical psychologists have aspired to present Jewish psychology as the "application of the divine utterance that we received at Mount Sinai,"[1] which they reveal with their psychological exegesis, all I wanted to do was to offer my readers an infrastructure of Jewish psychology that encompasses the multiple spheres of our lives and which relies on the pluralistic strength that is contained in the principle of *shivim panim laTorah* ("the Torah can be interpreted in seventy [that is, an infinite number of] ways"). Of course, psychological exegetes are nevertheless invited to use the infrastructural base I have built in order to develop additional, alternative versions that will be as imaginative as possible.

In this book, which was written after the psychology of Tzimtzum had already acquired many followers, I am simply explaining my thoughts, rather than seeking to prove them for the first time. I continue to touch on ideas I raised in earlier books on the secret of Tzimtzum, to which I refer all interested readers in the footnotes.

This book begins with an introduction explaining the position of Tzimtzum *vis-à-vis* psychodynamic psychology and the intellectual world on which it is predicated. The remaining four chapters discuss the four dimensions in which I see the impact of Tzimtzum: the intergenerational, intrapersonal, interpersonal, and suprapersonal dimensions.

As the book's title suggests, it is intended to serve as an introduction to the other books I have written. I hope it will be beneficial to a broad spectrum of therapists; to individuals who want to learn both how to lead and create for others a more fruitful

---

1. See, for example, M. Aboulafia, *HaGanan VeHaPri*, p. 18. Aboulafia presents the reader with a collection of principles serving as guidelines for a happy life. The principles, which are not organized according to areas of daily life, are written in the style of a traditional Jewish moralistic treatise (*sefer mussar*) and are based on his clinical experience (which relies on all the various Western techniques). To give a Jewish character to his principles, he cites traditional rabbinical sources.

life; and to the educated reader who is interested in an alternative to modern psychology and to the Christian world behind it.

I wish to thank the people who helped make this book available to the public. My thanks to Miri Mass for her initiative and for enthusiastically encouraging me to begin writing such an introduction to my work. I am grateful to my editor Amit Assis for having undertaken this difficult task and for illuminating, along the length and breadth of my written work, the various points that could chart a straight line and which could be accessible to intelligent readers without any need for superfluous justifications coming from someone who is cross-eyed. Many thanks to my daughter and student Michal Fachler for her advice regarding the work on this book. My appreciation goes to my students Dr. Baruch Kahana and Ruthie Gumbo, both of whom read the draft of the book and made important comments whose results can be seen here. My thanks to Baruch and Michal for the glossary that they compiled and which is presented here as an appendix. In light of the inner conviction that each individual's identity is shaped to a large extent by psychological language that he or she has internalized, this glossary is intended to help transform the theory of Tzimtzum into a living psychological language. In addition, I hope that the glossary will also serve as a kind of additional explanatory introduction to my other books. Nevertheless, I am the one who has written this book "at eye level" and who is looking the reader straight in the eye.

Lastly, I would like to thank Mark Elliott Shapiro for preparing the initial English translation of this work. Thanks are also due to the wonderful editorial staff of Maggid Books – Gila Fine, Tomi Mager, Avigayil Steiglitz, Ezra Margulies, Nechama Unterman, and Charlie Wollman – for the overwhelming love and devotion with which they handled the manuscript. It is only due to their hard work in practically rewriting the original text that the book has become accessible to the wider audience it will hopefully reach.

Chapter 1

Introduction: What is Tzimtzum?

Sixteenth-century Safed saw the blossoming of the world of Kabbala with the arrival of the Ari HaKadosh, Rabbi Isaac Luria. The Ari joined an imposing assembly of kabbalists under the leadership of Rabbi Moses Cordovero, and he soon became a foremost teacher of Kabbala. The kabbalistic concept of *Haatzala* (Inspiration), God's transfer of part of His spirit to the world, was already an integral component of the existing body of kabbalistic thought and continued to develop during and beyond the Ari's time. *Haatzala* depicts the creation of the world as a process taking place within God Himself. What is perceived in the Bible as a single act of creation is seen by Jewish mystics as a process of empowerment and is described in kabbalistic writings as a relationship between God the Creator and His creatures. In this relationship, each generation emerges from and receives something from the previous one, developing a constructive association between the two.

Building on the idea of *Haatzala* was the notion of Tzimtzum (self-contraction), propounded by the Ari and adopted by his disciples after his death. Like the entire body of kabbalistic thought, Tzimtzum featured prominently in hasidic writings. The narrative of God's creation of the world and His self-contraction is succinctly described by Rabbi Nachman of Bratslav:

> Because of His mercy, God created the world; He wanted to reveal His mercy and, if He had not created the world, to whom could He show His compassion? That is why He created the world in the following manner: The starting point is Emanation (*Atzilut*) and the end point is the center of the material world. When He wanted to create the world, there was no room in which to create it because He is infinite and occupies all space. That is why God contracted the light to the margins and, through this contraction (*Tzimtzum*), an empty space was created. Inside this available space, all six days of creation and all of the world's attributes were brought into being; in other words, inside this empty space, the world was created.[1]

The starting point for the world's creation is God's will to reveal His mercy. Here, however, arises a problem: since God is infinite and thus occupies the entire universe, there is simply no room for its creation! Accordingly, God creates within Himself a place where He contracts Himself, a place from which He

---

1. Nachman of Bratslav, *Likutei Moharan* (Jerusalem, 5740 [1979–1980]), 68:1.

removes His infinite light; inside this empty space, this vacuum, God creates the world.[2]

Tzimtzum generates the possibility for awareness of change, an awareness that does not reconstruct a previous situation but rather aspires to a new one. In light of the tendency of religions to encourage people to emulate God (*imitatio Dei*), this concept of God self-contracting could lead to an ideal model for human beings, according to which they contract themselves, while simultaneously giving to others, thereby mirroring God's creation of the world.

FREUD'S MYTHOLOGIES

In stark contrast to kabbalistic thought stands Sigmund Freud's depiction of the Oedipal individual. Freud transformed the story of Oedipus Rex from the well-known tale of the classical Greek playwright, Sophocles, to a now-familiar Western narrative, by placing Oedipus at the forefront of his theories. Let us briefly review Sophocles' famous drama before discussing Freud's conclusions:

---

2. A concept similar to the kabbalistic idea of Tzimtzum also appears in the philosophical writings of certain Christian thinkers from the fifteenth century onward. In the Christian version of the concept, the human world and the reality surrounding human beings are described as a self-contraction in relation to God's perfection. Rather than relating to Tzimtzum *per se*, these Creation theories pertain solely to human beings because their purpose is to explain the human possibility of choosing evil. The hasidic-kabbalistic approach is the complete opposite: Tzimtzum is the result of a desire to do good, not the result of a desire to enable the existence of evil. Whereas the Christian model is intended to help people come to terms with the existence of evil in the world, the hasidic concept of Tzimtzum can be seen as a positive model encouraging believers to emulate God who contracts Himself. For an extensive discussion of this point, see M. Rotenberg, *Hasidic Psychology* (New Brunswick, 2004), pp. 9–15.

Laius, King of Thebes, learns from an oracle about the fate of his son, who will one day kill his father and marry his mother; the king binds Oedipus' feet and orders a shepherd to hurl him from the peak of a mountain. Spared by the shepherd, who takes pity on him, Oedipus finds his way to the palace of Polybus, King of Corinth, who raises him as his son. After learning of his destiny, Oedipus escapes from the palace in order to avoid killing Polybus, believing him to be his father. On the road, he becomes involved in a dispute with someone and kills him, unaware that he has actually killed his biological father, Laius. Oedipus eventually arrives in Thebes, saves his mother, the Queen of Thebes, Jocasta, from the claws of the Sphinx, and marries her.

With his new rendering, Freud revived the tale as the basic underlying myth of Western culture, yet he gave it a distinctly new direction: the sexual craving of the child for his mother, accompanied by aggression toward and a desire to kill his father, with the result of intergenerational tension. In this new myth, a person's fate is not decreed by an oracle, but is rather to be found inside himself, an inborn element of the human personality. It is the sexual urge, which no person can resist – even by fleeing to Corinth.

> If *Oedipus Rex* moves a modern audience no less than it did the contemporary Greek one...there must be something which makes a voice within us ready to recognize the compelling force of destiny in the *Oedipus*...a factor of this kind is involved in the story of King Oedipus. His destiny moves us only because it might have been ours; because the oracle laid the same curse upon us before our birth as upon him. It is the fate of all of us, perhaps, to direct our first sexual

impulse toward our mother and our first hatred and our first murderous wish against our father.[3]

Assigning himself the role of oracle, Freud reveals to the members of modern Western society that intergenerational tension is their inevitable fate. This tension is thus elevated to the level of myth. Even if Sophocles does not move us as Freud claims he does, Freud has certainly moved us – so much so that there is hardly any aspect of Western culture which has not been deeply affected by the psychoanalytic myth of Oedipus. Although in Sophocles' myth only Oedipus is presented as facing his particular personal dilemma, Freud's psychoanalytic myth presents a scientific certainty; Freud's Oedipus is an Everyman. The psychoanalytic myth establishes an insoluble tension between the individual's sexual nature and his life's circumstances, his family, and his culture.

If Freud had merely created tension, however, it would have worked in two directions: just as the father is threatened by the son, so too the son is threatened by the father. If the tension were presented from both sides, alongside the fantasies of patricide we would also be hearing about fantasies of filicide; in other words, parallel to the Oedipus complex, we would also be hearing about the Laius complex. Yet Freud does more than just accentuate a myth; he points out where the solution lies. For Freud, the father's symbolic murder is the sole way for the son to become an adult, as inevitable as mythological fate. Out with the old and in with the new; the father must be done away with for the son to come into his own.

Interestingly, the German philosopher Georg Wilhelm Friedrich Hegel, who was born nearly a century before Freud,

---

3. S. Freud, *Complete Psychological Works*, vol. 4 (London, 1900), p. 262.

developed the concept of progress and existence by means of patricide. At the heart of Hegel's philosophy is the idea that the human spirit develops dialectically, meaning that an entity's survival is dependent upon its victory over another entity, producing a new, stronger entity. The two original warring entities are known as the *thesis* and *antithesis*, whereas the new entity, containing elements of both thesis and antithesis, yet contradicting both, is called the *synthesis*. This continuing process of thesis, antithesis, and synthesis perfects the human spirit, and the ongoing process of perfection expresses itself in both human civilization and in nature:

> The bud disappears when the blossom breaks through, and we might say that the former is refuted by the latter; in the same way, when the fruit comes, the blossom may be explained by a false form of the plant's existence, for the fruit appears as its true nature in place of the blossom. These stages are not merely differentiated, they supplant one another as being incompatible with one another... but one is as necessary as the other.[4]

Hegel presented truth as a concept that develops with time; every perception of truth exhausts itself, disintegrates, and is replaced by a succeeding one. This vision of progress and development parallels Freud's theory described above: a new spirit can develop only through the negation and erasure of the previous thesis, and the son can become an adult only at the price of erasing the father.

---

4. G.W.F. Hegel, *Hakdama LaFenomonologia Shel HaRuach*, translated and explained by Yirmiyahu Yovel (Jerusalem, 5756 [1995–1996]), pp. 47–48.

The roots of this approach in Western society are ancient.[5] In Greek mythology there are many instances where a generation of gods is created as the result of war and the destruction of the previous generation of gods. This mythological picture penetrated the Christian world, which dictated Europe's history for centuries. Paul, formerly Saul of Tarsus, the Jew who established Christianity, appears to follow this pattern. Paul's act can be seen as Oedipal: he killed the religion of the father (Judaism) in order to create from it the religion of the son (Christianity). This Oedipal act is also expressed in the very content of Christianity, where the religion's focus is shifted from the Father (God) to the Son (Jesus).

Similarly, we find traces of this idea in the nineteenth century. Charles Darwin's theory of evolution is a developmental approach that centers on the concept of the survival of the fittest, which represents a more advanced stage of a given species. The more developed species is able to overcome the lesser-developed species, and thus survives. Karl Marx also considered himself a disciple of Hegel; for Marx, however, historical progress is not an expression of the advancement of the human spirit, rather, the human spirit is an expression of real conflicts over the means of production. According to Marx, communism will triumph only after capitalism in its most extreme form has exhausted itself and has enraged the working class so much that the people are prepared to go to war against it.

We have presented here a brief outline of the development of dialectical thinking: the new vanquishes the old and the replacement is regarded as more desirable than its predecessor.

---

5. For a study that extensively surveys both the roots of the perception according to which history progresses through conflict and the broad application of that perception, see R.A. Nisbet, *Social Change and History* (New York, 1979). For a more extensive survey than the one appearing in this book, see my book: M. Rotenberg, *Rewriting the Self* (New Brunswick, 2004), pp. 72–93.

The philosophy of dialectics is totally unlike the warm, loving kabbalistic approach of Hasidism. In Hasidism, there is room for everybody. No one is pushed away, murdered, or negatively diminished. Whereas Freud assigns to each individual his specific fate from which he cannot escape, namely, a son's desire to kill his father in order to expand himself, Hasidism has created a living, breathing culture where all are encouraged to live life to its fullest, the old and young giving to and growing from each other. In addition, as we shall see, this culture even has certain methods for dealing with deviations from the social norm, including its own quasi-therapeutic customs.[6]

But how is this achieved?

THE GOD WHO CONTRACTS HIMSELF

I wish to outline here an alternative to the Oedipus model, an alternative which – inspired by the hasidic-midrashic tradition that developed in Europe during the advent of modernity – shall serve as a basis for a radically different therapeutic worldview. Hasidism posits a process of development in which intergenerational hierarchy does not give rise to conflict, and progress does not require war. Instead, Hasidism advances the possibility of a world based on intergenerational dialogue – between father and son and between teacher and student. Hasidism, with its intergenerational hierarchy, offers a process of development which need not generate a world of conflict in which progress requires war, advancing instead the possibility of a world based on intergenerational dialogue – between father and son and between teacher and student.

---

6. On hasidic therapeutic institutions, see my book: M. Rotenberg, *Hasidic Psychology*, and see also B. Kahana, *The Breaking [of the Vessels] and Their Repair as a Paradigm for Psychopathology and Psychotherapy* (PhD diss., Hebrew University of Jerusalem, 5765 [2004–2005]).

This alternative I am proposing to Hegelian dialectics follows Martin Buber's concept of dialogue, by which the two dialoguing parties exist side by side.[7] In the "I-Thou" relationship, the "I" and "Thou" remain intact and are not swallowed up in a dialectical process that must end in "I *or* Thou," that is, in a new entity that nullifies the previous one.[8] In the course of this book, I will show the ramifications of the "I-Thou" dialogic model on the relationship between past and present, therapist and patient, and human relationships in general.

Buber's dialogic approach has not been accepted in practice because it exists in a world where the dominant thinking is shaped by Hegelian dialectics. Instead of the dialectical principle, where one element replaces another, I am proposing a dialogic process where two seemingly opposing elements enable one another to grow.[9]

Let us return to the myth of Oedipus and compare it to the narrative of God's creation of the universe. Laius and Oedipus both attempt to evade their fate (Laius removes Oedipus from the palace,

---

7. See M. Buber, *BeSod Siaḥ: Al Adam VaAmidato Nokhaḥ HaHavaya* (Jerusalem, 5724 [1963–1964]), pp. 3–103.

8. S.H. Bergman, *HaFilosofia HaDialogit MiKierkegaard ad Buber* (Jerusalem, 1974), pp. 147–148.

9. However, I must point out that, in accordance with the dialogic formulation proposed here, "I and Thou" remain intact even at the negative level. Thus, although evil can serve as a "chair for good," to cite the Besht's famous saying, it does not become good; it contracts itself so that good can be derived from it: "The chair does not become a bench." According to the mistaken dialectical interpretation recently given to the popular concept "union of opposites," when evil becomes good, the reversal of Purim – "Cursed is Haman" to "Blessed is Mordechai" – is justified. However, this dialectical distortion of the *paradoxical* nature of midrashim runs the risk of deteriorating into something quite dangerous; according to that kind of thinking, "Heil Hitler" could eventually be justified, God forbid, on the grounds that, after all, the Holocaust contributed to the establishment of the State of Israel.

ordering his execution, while Oedipus tries to escape from the person he thinks is his real father). Both fail. Contrast their vain endeavors with God's decision to self-contract in order to make room for His creations, where He dwells in the world in all His glory, yet creates space for the work of His hands to grow and thrive. The starting point of God's Tzimtzum is not a decree of fate but rather a desire to reveal love, not a conflict between two entities but rather the desire of one of those entities to go beyond itself in order to meet the other. The hero of Tzimtzum is the father who understands that he cannot live alongside his child without contracting himself. Instead of distancing his son from him or trying to kill him, the father solves the problem by contracting himself in order to make room for the son; he thereby creates an open story, whose ending is not predetermined, a story that allows for the kind of dialogue Buber suggests. The father creates the change that enables the son to grow. Rather than having to preserve his existence by destroying his father, the son can live together with his father in peace.

In the course of this book, we will see how the concept of Tzimtzum can be realized in its different dimensions. In the second chapter, we will propose a model for intergenerational development, building on the foundations of Tzimtzum to establish an alternative to the dialectical Oedipus complex, in which father and son compete.

In the third chapter, we will propose the personal dimension of Tzimtzum as a model for relating to ourselves, to our urges, and to our past. Just as God's Tzimtzum leads to the creation of the world, the adoption of this principle can also direct us toward a personal process of positive change. We will offer midrash as an instrument for reinterpreting our personal history, a process of *teshuva* that does not cancel out the past.

Chapter four will move from the psychological sphere to the sociological one, showing how the concept of Tzimtzum can have a profound effect on society. We will describe an interpersonal relationship that can be created when individuals fulfill themselves in different ways, making room for a range of social ideals (for example, the mercantile tribe of Zebulun supporting the scholarly tribe of Issachar), rather than placing themselves at identical starting points from which they must compete with one another. Similarly, we will consider the capacity of society to contract itself and thereby include those who do not behave normatively. This model of a community whose members contract themselves is valid not only for an entire society but also for smaller groups, such as neighborhoods, business partnerships, or even married couples.

The fifth and final chapter will deal with the dimension that I term suprapersonal and it will touch on psychology's ability to allow for religious and mystical experiences, instead of seeing those experiences as manifestations of insanity that must be overcome so that the individual can be "cured." Just as people can peacefully coexist through dialogue, psychology can peacefully coexist with suprapersonal, religious worlds without compromising its scientific methods.

In this, I seek to suggest the possibility of a different kind of psychology, one that does not compete with other theories of the ideal personality, but rather learns how to live side by side with them.

Chapter 2

The Binding of Isaac:
The Intergenerational
Dimension of Tzimtzum

The family is the locus of our development as individuals, particularly in the early years of our life. In many cultures, it is described as a fraught environment, a battlefield. The Greeks have Oedipus, who kills his father and marries his mother; the Persians tell the story of King Rustum, who accidentally kills his son; Mesopotamian culture recalls a war between the gods and their young sons (also gods), who disturb their fathers' slumber. The tension between fathers and sons is universal and its various literary depictions bring it to a level of actual violence.[1] Each

---

1. L. Shelef, *Generations Apart* (New York, 1981).

culture has its own distinct way of presenting this intergenerational tension and the solution to the conflict.

Psychoanalysis assumes as its point of departure an insolvable, violent conflict between the father and the son. According to Freud, the father is a rigid tyrant who, fearing that his son will ultimately usurp him, demands total obedience and loyalty. The son, however, refuses to accept this authority, aspiring instead to develop his own individuality and autonomy. This is the crux of the Oedipal relationship: The authoritarian, aggressive patriarch inspires in his son a fear of castration (an element Freud adds to Sophocles' myth) which, in turn, arouses in the son an aggressive urge to murder his father.

Freud's Oedipal theory became so prevalent in the Western world, it engulfed the psychoanalytic field and became the basic model for coming of age. Western man's worldview requires that he be independent; patricide, or the cutting of the umbilical cord, allows him to become a free, autonomous individual. Sociologist Peter Berger hence describes patricide as a positive element in the biography of the average man:

> Many Americans seemingly spend years of their life... retelling over and over again (to themselves *and* to others) the story of what they have been and what they have become... and in this process killing their parents in a sacrificial ritual of the mind.... It is no wonder, incidentally, that the Freudian mythology of patricide has found ready credence in American society and especially in those recent middle-class segments of it to whom such rewriting of biographies is a social necessity of legitimizing one's hard-won status.[2]

---

2. P. Berger, *Invitation to Sociology* (New York, 1963), p. 60.

Patricide is not confined to the therapist-patient relationship or, indeed, to the private sphere. It is the model of revolutionary politics, one which determines the social power structure and creates a world that "belongs to the young"; the elderly, by this model, are sent to retirement homes, where they are, in a way, "buried alive." In a world where liberty is perceived as an essential characteristic of the human race, the hierarchy inherent in intergenerational relations becomes unbearable.

I wish to suggest an alternative model to the hierarchical father-son relationship, based on another foundational narrative of Western culture: the Binding of Isaac. This narrative, as central to Judaism as the Oedipus myth is to the Greeks, will serve as a prototype for the hasidic view of hierarchical and intergenerational relations. It is, as we shall see, a paradigm that adopts the idea of Tzimtzum and develops it into a model for interpersonal relations.

Both the Oedipus myth and the Binding of Isaac have the father-son relationship as their central theme. In addition, both narratives feature a great divine "Father," framing the dynamic between the divine and the human as a relationship between a Father-God and son-man. In the mythological story of Oedipus, the divine utterance appears as a decree to which men are subjected, regardless of their own desires. Throughout the tale, man seeks to escape his fate: Laius tries to kill his son Oedipus so that the latter will not kill him, while Oedipus escapes from the person he thinks is his father (Polybus) in order not to kill him. However, despite their attempts, both Laius and Oedipus fulfill their predestined fate. In Greek tragedy, the decree of fate is thus a kind of father figure, who ultimately always has his way.

When we examine the relationship between the divine and the human in the story of Oedipus, however, we discover that this underlying structure is contradicted by the story's plot. While in the father-son relationship, the son always has the upper hand (and kills the father), in the relationship between divine fate and human actions, fate will always triumph (Oedipus ends up killing his father against his will). Hence, while the story posits the defeat of the father by the son, its subtext presupposes the victory of the father.

In the Genesis narrative of the Binding of Isaac, God's words are not a decree of fate; they are a command. Fate leaves man no choice; he is stripped of his free will. In contrast, the command leaves the end of the story within human hands. The God who issues the command remains unchanged. But He contracts Himself before man, directing him and obligating him, while simultaneously offering him the freedom to disobey.

Here lies the major difference between the two narratives. On the one hand, according to the myth of Oedipus, man's fate is patricide. The foreknown passing of the elder generation and the succession of the younger one is translated into the story of a predetermined murder. The starting point of the Genesis story, on the other hand, is potential filicide. The father exercises his authority, his power, *vis-à-vis* the son. Some cultures would allow him, or even expect him, to make use of violence. Roman law, for instance, gave a father unlimited authority (*patria potestas*) over his children, which included the power to execute them.[3] Similarly, we find accounts from various cultures of kings who sacrifice their sons and daughters in order to obtain divine favors. The Bible, for example, relates the story of Meisha, King of Moab, who offers up his son in order to save his city from a siege (II Kings 3:26–27). In Greek mythology, Agamemnon immolates Iphigenia to the goddess Artemis, expecting the wind to start blowing again and enable his ships to sail to war against Troy. Both kings, Meisha and

---

3.   D. Bakan, *The Duality of Human Existence* (Boston, 1966).

Agamemnon, sacrifice their children to their respective deities in order to prosper and strengthen their royal status.

With regard to Abraham, the opposite is true: he seeks to bring children to the world and impart to them his connection with God. He forgoes this objective in an act of contraction when yielding to God's first command: "Take now thy son... and offer him there" (Gen. 22:2). Abraham's conduct is different from that of Laius. The latter does not seek to obey, but rather, to defend himself from the anger of the gods by attempting to kill his son.

However, Abraham's story does not end here. In abandoning his vision of a son who will outlive him, he also relinquishes his dream of having descendants. He surrenders this objective to his greater desire to fulfill the divine command. This forfeit is his mission. But then comes the second command: "Lay not thy hand upon the lad" (Gen. 22:12). Abraham must once again contract himself, abandon the purpose of his journey to Mount Moriah, and surrender the religious urge to fulfill the divine command. Certain midrashim underline Abraham's mixed impulses, torn between the conflicting demands of each injunction, even insisting on fulfilling at least part of the first command to sacrifice Isaac:

> Abraham: Let me strangle him.
> God: Lay not thy hand upon the lad.
> Abraham: Let me at least draw one drop of his blood...
> God: Neither do thou anything unto him.[4]

Even though the Midrash does not faithfully reflect the way Abraham is portrayed in the Bible, it provides a vivid representation of a devoutly religious individual who cannot forsake

---

4. Genesis Rabba 56:7.

his mission outright. Moreover, the existence of the second command necessarily implies a different form of divine behavior. God changes His request; He therefore reacts to human deeds.

Oedipus' story depicts an irresolvable conflict between the father and the son. The decree of fate places before both characters a clear dilemma: either the father or the son will die. This conflict represents the driving force behind the narrative. In terms of thesis and antithesis, it highlights a *contradiction*. In the story of the Binding of Isaac, in contrast, the two opposing forces stand side by side, bridging the tension that would otherwise exist between them. This relationship may be characterized as a *paradox.*

There is another significant difference between the mythical story and the biblical narrative. The mythical story is driven by a decree of fate, which posits that children will inevitably dislodge their own parents. The starting point of the biblical narrative, in contrast, is the difference in status between father and son. This difference does indeed create a hierarchy, but one that is not a decree of fate. The father avoids using force against his son, just as God refrains from ruling the world with inescapable decrees of fate. The story of the Binding of Isaac depicts one generation following in the footsteps of its predecessor; of a dialogue, rather than a conflict, between both generations. The concept of Tzimtzum enables both parties to change and coexist.

A FATHER'S TZIMTZUM

In Oedipus' story, the father Laius is not a central character. In contrast, both Abraham and Isaac, father and son, are protagonists in the story of the Binding of Isaac. Whereas the biblical account reduces Isaac's involvement in the narrative to silence, midrashic literature and *piyutim* (sacred poems) attempt to fill this void. In psychoanalytical therapy, the father is unchanging; he is necessarily a traumatizing figure. Consequently, the son has the difficult task of dealing with a traumatic past that determines his present. By contrast, I now wish to draw the picture of a religious father who, following the divine model of creation through self-contraction, contracts himself in order to raise his son. I will follow for this purpose in the footsteps of the Maggid of Mezeritch, the successor of the Baal Shem Tov (the Besht) at the head of the hasidic movement, who adopted numerous elements of the Ari's kabbalistic system to create an entire spiritual, social, and moral worldview.

We previously described dialectical theories (such as Marxism or Darwinism) as representing human relations in terms of a "zero-sum" game, in which one side's victory necessarily implies the other side's defeat. The kabbalistic notion of Tzimtzum is one in which power is granted to the other side; it contributes to the depiction of a world founded upon divine grace bestowed upon it in a process where God contracts Himself in order to grant power to mortals.

According to this kabbalistic system, the central interest is to give to the other party, as Rabbi Y.L. Ashlag writes in his introduction to the Book of Zohar:

> God created the world in order to provide pleasure and enjoyment to His creatures. Thus, we can deduce that God wants to have an influence on the beings He has created, that He is pleased to see the recipients of His goodness increase in number, that He very much wants them to multiply.[5]

The Maggid of Mezeritch explains that God's Tzimtzum was "essential for the world which, without this Tzimtzum, would have been

---

5. Y.L. Ashlag, *Mavo LeSefer HaZohar*, in: Y.L. Ashlag, *Sefer HaZohar Im Peirush HaSulam* (Jerusalem, 5715 [1954–1955]), pp. xxvii–xxviii.

unable to receive the infinite light…and would thus never have been capable of existing."[6]

Giving is not just a divine interest; it is also a basic human desire. Think, for example, of a writer or scientist who has been ordered not to share the fruits of her labors; obviously, she will suffer from her inability to give to others something of importance. Through the act of giving, we make life more enjoyable. Our personal happiness and satisfaction increase. In fact, giving is a major feature of the way many of us define ourselves – as professionals, parents, marriage partners, or simply as friends.[7]

The prevailing ethical code in Western society presupposes that we operate out of self-interest and compete with others in order to acquire more. This mindset does not seriously take into account the notion that giving constitutes a basic human desire. In contrast, according to the Ari's kabbalistic worldview and his depiction of God's Tzimtzum, the individual who gives to others has internalized a system in which the act of giving is a blessing that God bestows upon the world and upon each individual. While the former conflictual mindset dictates that we should act in accordance with our own interests (provided we do not harm others), we find here a hierarchical worldview in which individuals have an interest in the growth of those beneath them, and therefore, an incentive to contract themselves. This value system recognizes the existence of relationships based on acceptance and the act of giving, and appreciates its importance for the recipient as well as the giver.

According to the Maggid, God contracts Himself and reduces the intensity of His light (this is known as *Imum HaOr*, or

---

6. Dov Baer, Maggid of Mezeritch, *Maggid Devarav LeYaakov* (Lublin, 1927), p. 36.
7. For an expansion of this discussion, see my book: M. Rotenberg, *Between Rationality and Irrationality* (New Brunswick, 2005), pp. 100–101.

"dimming of the light") in order to communicate with man. He uses the metaphor of father and son to explain biblical expressions that present God anthropomorphically as a Being who can feel love, compassion, anger, and regret: "God contracted His light, as it were, like a father who contracts his intelligence and speaks in a childish language so that his young son will understand ... God contracted Himself for Israel's sake and did so out of love."[8] God performs this act of Tzimtzum to be able to interact with man. Hence in the context of a family, the father gives to his son, and thereby contracts himself, but with no desire to subsequently expand. Thus, divine action manifests itself in human behavior: man learns how to emulate God by adopting His patterns of behavior and then continuing on his own by granting power and giving to others.

It is clear, then, that the motif of divine Tzimtzum can be adopted at the human level; we can contract ourselves in order to focus on the needs of others. This is a process in which one party shows empathy for another:

> If we have to concentrate our thought on something that is essential to us, we must contract our thought substantially and not reflect on anything else; otherwise, our thoughts will become confused and we will then be unable to complete our consideration of that essential matter.[9]

Here is how the Maggid explains the transfer of cognitive knowledge from the rabbi to the student:

> If the rabbi wants to convey something from his vast body of knowledge to the student and the student is unable to

---

8. Dov Baer, Maggid of Mezeritch, *Maggid Devarav LeYaakov*, p. 9.
9. Ibid., p. 88.

receive all that knowledge, the rabbi contracts his intelligence by means of utterances and signs, in the same way that we use a funnel to pour a liquid from one vessel to another without spilling any of that liquid. The funnel contracts the flow of the liquid and thus the second vessel receives all of the liquid, none of which is spilled. Similarly, the rabbi contracts his intelligence with utterances and signs that the student can understand; in this way, the student is able to receive the rabbi's vast body of knowledge.[10]

The motif of Tzimtzum allows us to overcome a serious cognitive difficulty: how to inculcate the rabbi's or father's high level of knowledge to the student or son, who have lesser cognitive abilities. Although hasidic literature is no manual for therapeutic practice, it is possible to deduce educational strategies from the hasidic tradition. For example, the Besht used simple parables to disseminate his teachings. His disciples adopted this method, developing the art of the parable and storytelling into a primary pedagogic tool. The hasidic leader was thus required to address his audience in a language they could understand, instead of expecting the audience to raise itself to his level.

In the sphere of parenting, the motif of Tzimtzum demands that the father lower himself substantially, to reach the level of his son. The father must address the son as an equal, using simple words; in the Maggid's words, he must use "small words for his small son." Furthermore, when the father plays with his son, a role reversal occurs, enabling the latter to absorb his father's essential character traits. The Maggid also describes such a role reversal, in which the father stands in relation to his son in a way which mirrors God's relation with the beings of His creation:

---

10. Ibid., p. 47.

This is like a father who has a young son who wants to take a stick and ride it like a horse. Although the horse generally leads the rider, the son wants to lead the horse. Nevertheless, since the son enjoys this activity so much, his father helps him and gives him a stick in order to meet his son's wishes.[11]

The father contracts himself, forgoing his standing and role; he enables the son to imagine that he is riding a horse; sometimes he will even play the horse himself in order to please his young son. Interestingly enough, this surrender of his honor actually helps the father to realize his role as father, and as a teacher he fulfills himself through this act of educational love. Thus Tzimtzum is reciprocal. It does not suffice for the father to display love to the son. The son also enjoys the game, and gains further appreciation of his father. The same process which enables the father to draw closer to the son also allows the son to evolve in the direction of his father. Accordingly, as the son matures, he contracts himself in order to obey his father. This is known as Akedatic Tzimtzum, based on the term *Akedat Yitzhak* (the Binding of Isaac). Tzimtzum does not just occur at the cognitive level – whereby God lowers the level of His words so that mortals can understand them – but also at the emotional level. Tzimtzum enables interaction of mutual influence, where one can express himself and be present at the side of the other without any fear of being overshadowed or silenced. This risk exists when the meaning of divine Tzimtzum is abandoned. In a world that places paradigmatic importance upon self-fulfillment and encourages individuals to take pride in their own achievements, where the act of giving constitutes a deviation from normative behavior, the recipient is burdened with the need to discharge his debt, while the giver takes on the role of scornful creditor. According to a medieval

---

11. Ibid., p. 11.

thinker, "Gratitude is always mixed with shame...which gives one a feeling of being thwarted."[12] Such a system of values alienates the recipient from the giver in a way that prevents both parties from experiencing gratitude or mutual love.

Tzimtzum does more than just make room for empathy. It is not merely a process of role assumption whereby the father, as a fully developed individual, displays understanding toward his son;[13] it also constitutes a tangible act of giving from father to son.

Tzimtzum prompts the father to make some room in his personal space, which the son may enter. In this way, the former may be involved in the latter's life, yet without actively interfering. The father contracts himself and forms a mutual relationship with the son at the latter's level. This model contrasts with an intervention "from above," which the son may perceive as invasive. The love of the son toward the father and of the student for the teacher then constitutes a response, which trickles toward the father or teacher and instills them with pride and self-fulfillment.

The traditional children's game of hide-and-seek can help us understand the concept of Tzimtzum. The father hides, conceals himself, and allows the son to look for him. The father does not disappear entirely from the son's life, nor did God completely vanish from the world. When He contracted Himself, God left an impression – in kabbalistic terminology, a *reshimu* – through which the world could communicate with Him. The child remembers the father who is hiding and sets out to search for him. The father does not make his presence felt in the form of a stern demand; quite

---

12. Juan Luis Vives, cited by A.G. Zilburg: A.G. Zilburg, *A History of Medical Psychology* (New York, 1941), p. 193.
13. On this kind of activity, see my article: M. Rotenberg, "Conceptual and Methodological Notes on Affective and Cognitive Role-Taking (Sympathy and Empathy): An Illustrative Experiment with Delinquent and Non-Delinquent Boys," *Journal of Genetic Psychology* 125 (1974): 177–185.

the contrary, he effaces his presence and leaves only a memory of himself, a spark that will ignite a flame in the son's heart. This is his "inner light." In this way, the son reaches the father through his own efforts and of his own accord, without any pressure from the father.

THE TZADDIK

The hasidic community is not egalitarian. It does not ignore the natural human tendency for creating social structures, with its leaders and followers. The psychology of Tzimtzum allows for hierarchical relationships and identifies the potential inherent in them. From a position of leadership, the figure of authority can self-contract and enable growth. If we identify the possibilities inherent in hierarchical relationships, we can understand how attempting to ignore or cancel them can suppress a significant human need.

At the heart of Hasidism stands the spiritual figure of the tzaddik. The position of the tzaddik, or hasidic *rebbe*, in his community is more central than that of a mere rabbi, whose role is defined as a Torah educator and as a teacher of Jewish law. By placing the tzaddik at its center, hasidic society becomes a collaborator in his endeavors (akin to Buber's "I-Thou" utopian community).[14]

Later in this book, we shall deal with a model for interpersonal relationships rooted in the psychology of Tzimtzum. We will describe in greater detail the structure of the society which emerges from such a psychology. In the meantime, however, I want to focus on the model of the hierarchical relationship between the *rebbe* and the Hasid (often described as his student), and to compare it with what occurs in therapy.

---

14. M. Buber, *Netivot BeUtopia* (Tel Aviv, 1983), p. 185.

The psychoanalytical therapist, like the father or the rabbi, holds a position of authority in relation to the patient. The therapy process is built on the patient's descriptions of his life, his behavior, and his past. The patient is the subject of the conversation between himself and the therapist; of the two, it is the patient's life and emotions that are under discussion. In the course of the therapy, the patient puts forward his story and his emotions, while the therapist offers his interpretation. The therapy process is thus dialectical: the patient adopts the therapist's "correct" interpretation in place of his own.

In conservative Freudian theory, there exists an event hidden in the patient's past, which lies at the root of his complex. The therapist, accordingly, must bring to the fore this event in his interpretation of the patient's memories.[15] Proponents of narrative psychology, in contrast, will search for a creative and helpful interpretation, but do not consider whether it reflects the genuine truth.[16] What is common to both the past- and future-oriented approaches is that they grant the therapist the privilege of providing the "correct" interpretation for the patient. Advocates of both approaches conceive the dialectical therapist-patient relationship in similar terms: the therapist will undertake an act of quasi-patricide *vis-à-vis* the patient's perception of his own past and substitute it with his own interpretation. Thus, in Hegelian terms, the new, "healthy" interpretation supplants the old, sick, and withered one.

I wish to put forward a dialogic model for the therapist-patient relationship, in which the former makes use of his authoritative position in order to contract himself and leave room within which the latter may develop. This alternative discards the interpretive conflict and exploitative relationship which characterize

---

15. R. Schafer, *The Analytic Attitude* (New York, 1983).
16. D.E. Spence, *Narrative Truth and Historical Truth* (New York, 1982).

conservative Freudian theories.[17] I detect this model in the figure of the tzaddik as depicted in hasidic writings.

The source of the word tzaddik is *tzedek*, justice: the tzaddik is the one who actualizes spiritual and divine justice and reveals their unique qualities. To the tzaddik's exalted status, Hasidism adds the idea of social commitment. Hence the Besht's statement – in light of the verse, "The righteous man flourishes like the palm tree: he grows like a cedar of Lebanon" (Ps. 92:13) – that the tzaddik who is like the palm tree is preferable to the one who is like a cedar, since the former bears fruit and benefits his environment by dedicating his righteousness to helping others; whereas the latter might have a strong trunk and reach considerable heights, but his fruit does not contribute to his surroundings. Rabbi Jacob Joseph of Polonne distinguishes between the righteousness displayed by Noah, who saves himself from the Flood, and the righteousness of Abraham, who argues with God in order to rescue the people of Sodom.[18] Similarly, Rabbi Menahem Mendel of Kotzk distinguishes between the *tzaddik in peltz*, which, in Yiddish, designates a tzaddik who wraps himself in a fur coat and stays warm, and the tzaddik who buys wood in order to kindle a fire, and thereby provides heat for the entire community.[19] The latter displays the attributes of an eiderdown blanket, which absorbs body heat and then returns it in order to warm us.

How does the tzaddik help others? According to Buber, the tzaddik teaches us how to manage our lives in a way that will free our souls, and trains us to reinforce the soul so that it can

---

17. In the past, I have described the difference between dialectical and dialogic therapy. On the difference between describing a therapeutic conversation as interaction and describing it as a transaction, see my book: M. Rotenberg, *Between Rationality and Irrationality*.
18. See S.H. Dresner, *The Zaddik* (New York, 1960), p. 153.
19. M. Buber, *Or HaGanuz: Sippurei Ḥasidim* (Tel Aviv, 1976), p. 430.

contend with its lot. At times, the tzaddik knows how to lead us by the hand so that we may dare to continue along the road without him. He does not do, in our stead, what we ourselves are capable of.[20] The tzaddik is not just a savior who provides the Hasid, his follower, with the "right answer" for dealing with the challenges of life; he also clears a path that the follower can tread on his own. The leaders of Hasidism stress the importance of humility in constructing the image of the tzaddik. His humility enables the tzaddik to make room for those among his followers who have strayed from the accepted spiritual path in Jewish society. He does not reject them; rather, he makes room for them, and enables them to undergo a change that will bring them back to the patterns of normative behavior.

This function of the tzaddik is illustrated in a parable told by Rabbi Jacob Joseph of Polonne about a prodigal son who is returned to his father.[21] In this tale, the tzaddik is depicted as a living example of Tzimtzum. A prince is sent by his father to a village and does not return. The king dispatches his ministers to find him and bring him back to the palace. But the ministers' efforts prove fruitless, since, in the meantime, the prince has mixed with the villagers, learned their ways, and forgotten his royal pattern of conduct. One of the ministers decides to remove his magnificent attire and to dress like a common villager. He succeeds in finding the prince and returns him to his father. This tale, which became one of Rabbi Jacob Joseph's most celebrated parables and has been told and retold in many different versions, illustrates ideas which he and his followers considered of paramount importance.

The parable instructs the king's ministers (the tzaddikim, who are the ministers of God, the King of the Universe) to remove

---

20. Ibid., pp. 15–16.
21. On this story and for a discussion of it, see S.H. Dresner, *The Zaddik*, p. 177.

their royal attire, dress like ordinary people, and set out for the villages. There, they will draw closer to the masses and lead them back toward their heavenly Father. Rabbi Nachman of Bratslav, the Besht's great-grandson, uses a parable with a similar plot, but of even greater interest to us. This story reduces the considerable distance between the king and the prince: instead of a cultural gap (between the palace and the village), we witness a confrontation between the normal and the psychotic. Therefore, Rabbi Nachman's parable may prove useful in the construction of a model for psychological therapy. The story is quoted here in the version presented by Eliezer Steinman:

> A prince lost his mind and began to think of himself as a turkey. He sat naked under the table, refraining from all food except for raw oatmeal, which he would place in his mouth and eat …. The king his father summoned all the physicians in the kingdom to heal his son but none of them was able to come up with a cure. One day a wise man appeared before the king and said to him, "I will cure your son."
>
> The wise man immediately undressed and, sitting down under the table beside the prince, began to gather grains of oatmeal, which he put into his mouth. The prince asked him, "Who are you and what are you doing here?" The wise man replied with a question: "And who are you and what are you doing here?" "I am a turkey," said the prince. "And so am I," rejoined the wise man. The two turkeys sat under the table side by side until they became accustomed to one another.
>
> Seeing that the prince had become accustomed to his presence, the wise man motioned that he be given a robe. Putting on the robe, he turned to the prince, saying, "Do you think that a turkey is not entitled to wear a robe?

It is entitled to do so and that does not mean that it stops being a turkey." After pondering the wise man's words for a while, the prince also agreed to wear a robe. A few days later, the wise man asked for a pair of pants and, after putting them on, he asked the prince, "Do you think that a turkey is not entitled to wear pants?" The prince admitted that a turkey could wear pants and he also put on a pair of pants. Eventually, both the wise man and the prince were fully dressed.

Then the wise man requested human food and asked the prince whether a turkey had to sit under the table. They both concluded that a turkey could go wherever it wanted and that this was perfectly acceptable. The prince then began to walk about, to eat, and to act like an ordinary human being.[22]

In this parable, presented here almost in its entirety, the wise man conducts a therapeutic process as a dialogic therapist engaged in Tzimtzum. The therapist does not seek to make the prince acknowledge that he is not a turkey. The narrator does not disclose the prince's mindset, but engages instead from the point of view of society. Even though the prince ultimately behaves like a man, he may still believe he is a turkey. The therapist's intention is not to conduct a dialectical therapeutic process in the course of which he will replace the prince's self-awareness. The wise man has a different strategy. He uses the same language as the patient and even identifies with him. The conversation between the two is carried out at the level of the patient; the therapist identifies with him and even accepts his way of life. It is possible that this move

---

22. E. Steinman, *Kitvei Rabbi Nachman MiBratslav* (Tel Aviv, 1951), p. 157.

even has some sort of internal effect on the therapist. Nevertheless, he does not sever his ties with the normative world: he is still
capable of hinting to the people who are above the table that they
should throw them some clothes.

Soon after I started out as a therapist, I encountered a case
where this kind of "therapy" was successfully applied. A young man
arrived at the hospital department where I was interning. He had
been studying for his exams when he suddenly had an attack in
which he felt compelled to ask questions; the compulsion was so
serious that he found it extremely difficult to continue with his
daily routine. The medical team tried to take his mind off these
questions in several ways. Because of the patient's musical inclinations, one of the psychiatrists had the patient join him in a
guitar lesson during which his need to ask questions somewhat
diminished. The next stage of treatment was handled not by the
treatment team, but rather by an accordionist who had come to
the institution as a volunteer to entertain the patients. The accordionist, who was from the same country as the young patient,
was of the same age, and even looked very much like him, readily
accepted the challenge. In addition to teaching him how to play
the accordion, the volunteer also enabled the patient to return
to a normative lifestyle. The patient subsequently moved in with
the volunteer, began to dress like him, and adopted the same
hairstyle; they eventually became partners in the music business
and the entertainment scene. In the course of the therapy process,
the "therapist" managed to reach a point where the patient could
identify with him; the volunteer was then able to "befriend" the
patient and to raise him up "from under the table."

Rabbi Nachman's tale is not the only case of "emotional
therapy" where the therapist acknowledges the patient's world. The
"descent of the tzaddik" is a familiar theme in Hasidism; it is an act

in which the tzaddik descends from his lofty spiritual heights in order to enter a place where there are people with whom he wants to establish contact and whom he wishes to help. In the study of Hasidism, the motif of the descent of the tzaddik is carefully examined in relation to the messianism of Shabbetai Tzvi, who maintained that the Messiah must sin in order to achieve redemption.[23] Here I wish to discuss the usefulness of the tzaddik's descent as a therapeutic act *vis-à-vis* others in his community.

Elsewhere, Rabbi Nachman describes the motif in more kabbalistic terms, and considers the descent to be the way in which the tzaddik enters the space from which God contracted Himself in the course of the creation of the universe. According to Rabbi Nachman, this empty space is a dangerous place from which God seems absent. The tzaddik descends into such depths in order to raise the souls that have fallen into them.[24]

In Rabbi Nachman's account, the tzaddik descends into places where there are no answers to the questions he faces. He is confronted with questions that he cannot answer. Rabbi Nachman concludes that the tzaddik can raise the souls that have fallen into the available space only by remaining silent. Unlike speech, with which the world was created, silence represents the empty space, the place of Tzimtzum. The tzaddik must contract himself into silence. In order to raise the souls, he must neither speak nor answer questions. Thus, Rabbi Nachman prevents his tzaddik from functioning as a dialectical therapist who provides the "correct" solution.

---

23. See G. Scholem, *Major Trends in Jewish Mysticism* (New York, 1941) and *The Messianic Idea in Judaism*; see also M. Piekarz, *Bimei Tzemiḥat HaḤasidut* (Jerusalem, 1978) and J. Weiss, "The Beginnings of Hasidism," in: Rubinstein, A., ed., *Perakim BeTorat HaḤasidut UVeToldoteha* (Jerusalem: 5738 [1977–1978]), pp. 46–105.
24. Nachman of Bratslav, *Likutei Moharan* (141) 64.

TZIMTZUM OR DIAGNOSIS?

Psychologist R.D. Laing considers conflict to be the beginning of the psychological diagnosis. A conflict arises when someone claims to be the Messiah, or Napoleon, or a turkey, and society thinks differently. The therapist, as society's representative, then offers a diagnosis which will separate this individual from the rest of society.[25] The conflict leads us to perceive this person as "abnormal," and to mark him with a label that removes him from the rest of us. After failing to resolve its conflict with the individual, society labels him as distinct through the process of diagnosis. The diagnostic system is therefore based on a clear, firm picture of what is "correct," and can exclude anyone who does not meet the criteria of "correctness."

In order to prevent society from using a psychological diagnosis as a weapon in its war against deviations from the norm, Laing suggests that we compare diagnosis to the study of old manuscripts.[26] A scholar deciphers ancient texts with great difficulty because they are written in a foreign language. But he would never claim that the authors of the manuscripts were insane. Rather, he blames himself for not yet possessing the analytical tools for dealing with the material. The same could be said concerning the psychologist, who examines a patient behaving bizarrely. If such a model were used for diagnosis, the therapist would not see himself as someone standing on the solid grounds of "correctness." Indeed, therapy is a process in which the therapist can undergo a change if he is willing to learn about himself from his patient.[27]

---

25. R.D. Laing, *The Divided Self* (Middlesex, 1965), p. 36.
26. Ibid., p. 31.
27. Inspired by Buber's thought, M.S. Friedman recommends this kind of therapeutic praxis; see his *Martin Buber: The Life of Dialogue* (New York, 1971), p. 186. On this process of change within the context of interpretation, see

Such relationships, which hover between the normal and the deviant, can exist in an interpretive world where, as the Besht notes, "Evil is a chair for good."[28] Here is how Rabbi Yehiel Michel of Zlotshov explains the passage in the Mishna: "Who is wise? He who learns from every person" (Avot 4:1): "We must learn not only from educated people but from everyone. Even from the uneducated and even from the wicked you can learn how to conduct yourself."[29]

In my early clinical experience, I saw a young man in his late twenties who was already very knowledgeable about psychiatric therapy. He came to my office after having experienced a serious personal crisis and introduced himself as the Messiah. In accordance with accepted diagnostic tools, one could point to the differences between my patient and normative society and thereby conclude that he was insane. I began to consider the basic elements in his "madness" that the two of us shared to an extent. I told

---

Buber, who, beyond the creation of empathy toward the object being observed, attaches immense importance to dialogue:

> Empathy means, if anything, to glide with one's own feeling into the dynamic structure of an object, a pillar or a crystal or the branch of a tree, or even of an animal or a man, and as it were to trace it from within, understanding the formation and motoriality of the object with the perception of one's own muscles; it means to "transpose" oneself over there and in there. Thus it means the exclusion of one's own concreteness, the extinguishing of the actual situation of life, the absorption in pure aestheticism of the reality in which one participates. Inclusion is the opposite of this. It is the extension of one's own concreteness, the fulfillment of the actual situation of life, the complete presence of the reality in which one participates. Its elements are, first, a relation, of no matter what kind, between two persons; second, an event experienced by them in common. (M. Buber, *Between Man and Man* [New York, 1967], p. 97)

28. I. Baal Shem Tov, *Keter Shem Tov* (Jerusalem, 1975), p. 8.
29. Cited in Buber, *Or HaGanuz*, p. 144.

him that it is a normal human tendency to either ignore painful thoughts or to distract your mind from them when you find it hard to be yourself. I also told him that, in some cases, a person in such a situation will want to be someone else who has extraordinary powers and who is capable of saving humanity. The understanding that all people, including myself, can at times think that they are, in one way or another, the Messiah, helped my patient to deal with his crisis without having to deal with the painful thought that he was "insane." In therapy, this approach is known as "inclusive diagnosis," where the therapist accentuates similarities, rather than differences, between the patient and "normative" people.

MUTUAL EMULATION AND ḤUTZPA

The difference between "sanity" and "insanity" is the difference between being able and unable to contain varied self-images, to control them, and to live with them. This kind of approach can help us accept those who do not behave as we do. Hasidism grants its leaders certain tools that enable them to approach social deviations from a position that does not merely seek to impose a "correct" model of conduct by defining a deviation as "incorrect." Hasidic leaders are expected to consider deviations from the norm as a challenge they must deal with as leaders. Rabbi Jacob Joseph of Polonne provides an interesting interpretation of the biblical verses in which the Torah commands that lost possessions be returned to their owners. Deviations from the norm are described there as a lost possession; spiritual leaders are commanded to embrace the deviation and to study it as an expression of their own defects. Only then can they return the lost possession to its owner:

> "And if thy brother be not nigh unto thee, and thou know him not, then thou shalt bring it home to thy house, and it shall be with thee until thy brother require it, and thou shalt

restore it to him" (Deut. 22:2). "And if thy brother be not nigh unto thee": You must search your soul and seek out this defect. "... And thou know him not": Because you thought that you did not have this defect (although you really do have it), you did not regard the other person as your brother and you were not close to him; nonetheless, he is "thy brother." "... Then thou shalt bring it home to thy house": You must abandon all your other duties and seclude yourself so that you can study this defect inside your house, that is, this defect which is inside you. You must continually contemplate this sin which you saw in your brother but which is also in you. "... Until thy brother require it, and thou shalt restore it to him": After your soul-searching, you will discover that he is your brother because he and you have committed the same sin. You must atone for this sin, which is also in you, and only then can you help your brother atone for his sin.[30]

Tzimtzum enables a two-way relationship in which the therapist does not represent what is "correct" emotionally, that is, the emotional standard of correctness to which the patient is supposed to aspire. Instead, the therapist undergoes the process of therapy alongside the patient. In this model of therapy, the therapist is akin to a father or teacher; he is a therapist but not one who "influences." Rather, he himself undergoes a change in the process of therapy. This is also an educational process, and as we will see below, he is also influenced by the person he is teaching (namely, the patient). This is known in therapy as the "double mirror." Similarly, the hasidic rebbe makes no assumptions about the individual he is guiding. He too undergoes self-evaluation, and grows together with his follower.

---

30. Jacob Joseph of Polonne, *Toldot Yaakov Yosef* (Jerusalem, 1963), p. 687.

The Besht demands that the tzaddik look into the mirror and learn from what he sees, while dealing with the sinner. He requires that the tzaddik see himself in the sinner:

> If you see a sin being committed or hear about a sin having been committed, you must admit to yourself that you also have traces of that sin and you must resolve to correct your behavior.... By recognizing the sinner as your brother, you can help him to correct his ways. Furthermore, by recognizing him as your brother, you are in effect saying that we are all part of the same family, you are promoting unity and you are turning evil into good.[31]

The Besht demands that the tzaddik who detects sin in his fellow man should regard himself as tainted with traces of that very sin, and must therefore aspire to correct his ways. In this way, the sinner will also correct *his* ways. Although it is difficult to understand the logic of this demand, it did not represent an isolated and bewildering statement; indeed, his disciples followed this instruction.[32]

---

31. I. Baal Shem Tov, *Keter Shem Tov*, p. 21.
32. Rabbi Jacob Joseph of Polonne interprets the rabbinical saying, "Who is truly wise? One who learns from everybody" (Pirkei Avot 4:1) with the help of the mirror parable: "A truly wise person is one who learns from everybody and this is like looking in the mirror. You can see your blemishes in the mirror; similarly, others serve as a mirror and you can see your blemishes by looking at the blemishes in others" (*Toldot Yaakov Yosef,* p. 259). For a more miraculous interpretation of looking in the mirror, see the tale that is cited by Buber and which concerns Rabbi Zusya of Hanipoli:
    Once Rabbi Zusya came to an inn, and on the forehead of the innkeeper he saw long years of sin. For a while he neither spoke nor moved. But when he was alone in the room which had been assigned to him, the shudder of vicarious experience overcame him in the midst of singing psalms and he cried aloud: "Zusya, Zusya, you wicked man!

The tzaddik does not react to sinful behavior by stressing the difference between his own conduct and the sinner's. On the contrary, he examines his own inner being in order to find those very same sins. He therefore puts himself in the sinner's shoes, places aside his own righteousness, and does not distance himself from the transgressor. The tendency to self-righteousness when confronted with what we identify as deviant behavior becomes instead self-criticism that refines the character of the tzaddik and enables him to identify a certain degree of deviousness within himself.[33]

From this place, the tzaddik can communicate with the sinner in a way that emphasizes the similarity between both characters, rather than the former's superiority. The tzaddik does not react to sin with a sense of self-righteousness and incredulity. As a leader, he avoids adopting an arrogant attitude toward his followers and turns the struggle against sin into an arena of activities that attracts the attention of his people.

In directing his criticism toward himself, the tzaddik embarks on an introspective journey. As he "imitates" the transgressor, he unearths and confronts the sinner within himself. In contrast with the accepted, unidirectional educational idea of role-model imitation, where the student imitates the teacher, the process the Besht advocates is a two-way imitation that we term

---

What have you done! There is no lie that failed to tempt you, and no crime that you have not committed. Zusya, foolish, erring man, what will be the end of this?" Then he enumerated the sins of the inn-keeper, giving the time and place of each, and his own, and sobbed. The inn-keeper had quietly followed this strange man. He stood at the door and heard him. First he was seized with dull dismay, but then penitence and grace were lit within him, and he woke to God. (M. Buber, *Or HaGanuz*, p. 224)

33. For examples of such self-interpretation, see N. Lederberg, *Sod HaDaat: Demuto HaRuḥanit VeHanhagato HaḤevratit Shel Rabbi Yisrael Baal Shem Tov* (Jerusalem, 5767 [2006–2007]), pp. 84–94.

"mutual emulation." Mutual emulation works two ways because the tzaddik simultaneously emulates and is emulated: he emulates the sinner and, in doing so, turns himself into a role model that the general public takes as an example.

The tzaddik is an influential role model because he changes within the dynamics of the relationship between himself and his public. We therefore do not have a static model that the student is expected to imitate. The tzaddik undergoes an emotional process, contracting himself following the encounter with the sinner. He thereby avoids the sense of arrogance that may arise in every hierarchical system, and makes room emotionally for the other person to approach him. As the ideal social model, the tzaddik undergoes change in his contact with each person. He is not a passive symbol to be blindly imitated.

The process of mutual emulation does not end with the tzaddik's descent. The concept of mutual emulation depicts for us a world of mirrors in which there is shared influence between father and son, God and man, and tzaddik and follower. We can therefore expect the son to be able to influence his father. The following words of the Maggid, that are intended to encourage people to behave in a humble, self-contracting manner in imitation of God, provide a perfect example of such a dynamic.

> When we look in a mirror and strike a strong pose, our mirror image does the same. This is also true for our relationship with God: God reacts to us in accordance with the way we act in His presence. If we act in a true manner and remember that we originated as a tiny drop of foul-smelling semen, God will contract Himself in dealing with us so that we will have the strength to stand in His presence. However, if we act arrogantly, it stands to reason that God will act toward us in all His greatness. No mortal has the strength to stand

before God's greatness; we can only stand before Him if He contracts Himself.... Thus, you must behave humbly and be humble so that God will contract Himself and will descend, as it were, to your level, just like a father who sees his son playing with walnuts. Because of the love he bears toward the son, the father will join in the game, even though such activity is childish in the father's eyes. Nonetheless, because of the love he bears toward the son and because he wants to derive joy from the child, the father contracts his higher level of wisdom and descends to his son's lower level so that the child will have the strength to stand before his father. However, if the father acts in accordance with his higher level of wisdom, the son will not have the strength to stand before his father and the father, for his part, will be unable to derive joy from his son.[34]

To paraphrase the Maggid, we must imitate God's Tzimtzum and act humbly so that God will, as it were, emulate us and contract His blessing in a way that will enable us to receive it. This is also the manner in which the tzaddik receives the inspiration of the Divine Presence: "If the tzaddik behaves humbly and regards himself as a creature of no importance... when he thinks of himself as an insignificant creature and contracts himself, God will also contract His Divine Presence and will cause that Presence to hover above the tzaddik."[35] The driving force in this image is our behavior, that is, the extent to which we imitate God's qualities.

---

34. Dov Baer, Maggid of Mezeritch, *Maggid Devarav LeYaakov*, p. 63.
35. Ibid., p. 86.

There is a surprising reversal to this argument: instead of God influencing us, we are influencing Him. This dynamic is also witnessed in Abraham's debate with God over the fate of Sodom. Abraham questions God: "Shall not the Judge of all the earth do justly?" (Gen. 18:25). He is not speaking provocatively, but rather out of deference to God's image. Abraham is emulating God; only after donning His robe of justice does Abraham "accuse" God of acting unjustly. In this debate, God accepts this outburst of *ḥutzpa*. As the Talmud puts it, "Audacity (*ḥutzpa*) even before Heaven can achieve results" (Sanhedrin 105a).

Abraham appears here, in a sense, as God's son, as if he could take God's place. Abraham thus feels that he can assertively question God and even prompt Him to change His mind. A similar situation is offered in the famous story in the Talmud in which Ḥoni the Circle Maker "forces" God to bring down rain. Shimon b. Shettaḥ justifies Ḥoni's audacity in that tale and tells us why God does not object to such behavior:

> Shimon b. Shettaḥ sent him a message: "Were it not for Ḥoni, I would have to excommunicate you. However, I cannot decree any punishment for you. Although you are acting in a sinful manner, you are behaving like a son who is doing what his father wants him to do, as it is written: 'Let thy father and thy mother be glad, and let her that bore thee rejoice' (Prov. 23:25)." (Mishna Taanit 3:8)

The purpose of such *ḥutzpa* is not patricide; it is intended to draw the father's attention to the son. The son wants the father to contract himself and make room for him. According to Freudian thought, audacity is the manifestation of a repressed urge to kill one's father. I believe, on the other hand, that when a son behaves aggressively toward his father, he does not wish to kill him. Rather, he wants his father to notice him. If the father is able to contain these displays of *ḥutzpa* without compromising his own standing, he can channel them to respond to the son's demand and make room for him.

Chapter 3

Teshuva:
The Intrapersonal Dimension of Tzimtzum

The theory of Tzimtzum perceives human beings as having both a spiritual side and a physical one which are in dialogue with one another. The spiritual makes room for the physical, granting it legitimacy, and even a value of its own. In turn, the physical side dedicates itself exclusively to constructive, creative activity by contracting itself. Together they create an arrangement in which the material and the spiritual are not in competition, but rather complement each other. In this chapter, we will explore this idea and try to understand how a person can bring about *teshuva* using Tzimtzum. We will also consider using Tzimtzum as a meaningful alternative to mainstream psychodynamic therapy.

The Hebrew words *yetzer* (urge) and *yetzira* (creativity) are derived from the same root. In the word *vayitzer*, "He [God] created" (Gen. 2:7), the letter *yod* appears twice consecutively. The Midrash comments on this repetition, claiming that each *yod* stands for the word *yetzer*, and that this alludes to the two inclinations present in each human being: the *yetzer hatov* (our good urge or impulse) and the *yetzer hara* (our evil urge or impulse).[1] Sexual desire is not described as the root of all evil but rather as potential that we can use either for good or for evil. To illustrate this last point, the Talmud relates a story that describes an attempt to abolish all sexual impulses, a venture that leads to the suspension of all reproductive activity in the world (Yoma 69b and Sanhedrin 64a).

Judaism neutralizes the threat that the *yetzer hara* represents by contracting and subduing it. The Talmud advises on this subject: "If you meet this villain [the *yetzer hara*], take him to a house of Jewish study" (Kiddushin 30b). The *yetzer hara* is an energy that should not be regarded as a threat, but which should instead be harnessed for good: for creative spiritual activity (the study of Torah) or for creative physical activity (conjugal relations). The Besht develops the idea of contracting the *yetzer hara* and recommends, with both humor and intent, the following strategy, which is described in the form of a parable:

> Who is the hero who controls his evil impulse?... Let us take an example from the ways of the world. A person is in a room guarding a valuable possession; on hearing a thief approach, he raises a shout and the thief runs away. However, another person in the same situation will prepare chains beforehand; on hearing the thief approach, he will pounce on the thief and take him prisoner. The same can be said

about tzaddikim. Some of them do not allow any question-able thought to enter their heart or mind, while there are those who take that questionable or evil thought and sub-jugate it in their worship of God. Thus, when answering the question "Who is the hero...?" we should really consider those who are able to capture their *yetzer hara* and use it in the service of God.[2]

The Besht advises his adherents to make room for their *yetzer hara* so that it can be employed for creative activity. Here we have a case of mutual Tzimtzum: the spiritual side contracts itself in order to make room for the *yetzer hara*, while the *yetzer hara* contracts itself so that it can fulfill a constructive, creative purpose.

The Besht stresses that evil is not an independent entity: "The only unique entity is the Divine Presence; how can it contain two totally opposite things – good and evil? Because evil is a chair for good."[3] From such a monistic perspective, the abnormal element in a person can be interpreted as a voice crying out for correction and growth. This possibility is contained in the Besht's commentary on the verse, "Depart from evil and do good" (Ps. 37:27): "We must transform evil into good."[4]

In order to understand how Tzimtzum can serve us in the process of *teshuva*, we must examine the psychoanalytical concept of personality, which is based on conflict. On one side of the conflict are our physical urges, while on the other are the demands made by society. Freud describes this con-flict as a battle between the principle of pleasure, which is the

2. I. Baal Shem Tov, *Keter Shem Tov*, p. 37.
3. I. Baal Shem Tov, *Keter Shem Tov*, p. 8.
4. Ibid., p. 15.

assumption that all humans seek pleasure, and the principle of reality, which represents the behavior that is expected of an individual in any given society. According to Freud, the optimal situation is where the reality principle overcomes and replaces the pleasure principle, meaning that our behavior is suited to the reality of our lives.

This philosophy of conflict did not originate with psychoanalysis. Psychoanalysis is only the secular, modern version of the traditional Christian conflict between, on the one hand, the sexual urges of the physical world and, on the other, the spiritual world. Disengaging itself from physicality, Christianity perceived sexual abstinence as a prerequisite for religious excellence. It viewed sexual activity as the complete opposite of spiritual activity. The notion that sexuality is opposed to everything that is lofty in the human being is possible only if we regard it as purely physical. Judaism, in contrast, condemns sexual abstinence, seeking instead to employ the physical in the service of the spiritual.[5]

Following in the footsteps of the teachers of Hasidism, we can develop the model of Tzimtzum and envisage a process of *teshuva* through which we mature by harnessing the *yetzer hara* for positive change. This transformation offers the opportunity for a therapeutic process that takes place within each person.

---

5. For example, our Sages note that the Tanna Ben Azzai never married. The present quotation appears after a commentary attributed to Ben Azzai regarding the importance of the value of having children, and he is referred to as a person who did not practice what he preached. Ben Azzai apologizes for his preference for a life of Torah study over family life, describing his preference in terms of passionate desire rather than in terms of values: "What can I do? My soul has a passionate desire for Torah" (Tosefta, Yevamot 8:5).

ELEVATION OF THE SPARKS

Even a simple personal crisis contains the potential for spiritual growth. In order to achieve such success, there is a need for interpretation. This transformation plays a crucial role in the hasidic concept of the "elevation of the sparks" (*Haalaat Nitzotzot*). Kabbalistic Hasidism attributes the existence of apparent evil to the primordial "breaking of the vessels" (*Shevirat HaKelim*) that occurred during the process of divine Tzimtzum by which God created the world. The Ari describes how the act of giving, which is compared to light, exceeded the capacity of the vessels, which were therefore shattered. The divine sparks (*nitzotzot*), the essential constituents of goodness, were mixed with shells (*kelipot*), which are the essential constituents of apparent evil. This kabbalistic theory bestows upon man the responsibility for "correction" (*Tikkun*), that is, the restoration of the divine order through the "elevation of the sparks."

Our role on earth is to turn whatever appears to be evil into goodness through the medium of interpretation. We must attribute heavenly significance to our earthly existence: to eating, working, sexuality, and the simple joy of living. On this point, the Besht notes: "This is an important principle: everything in this world contains the divine sparks. There is nothing in this world that is devoid of these sparks – not even trees and rocks. There are even the sparks from the breaking of the vessels in everything we do, even in the sins we commit."[6] According to the Besht, all events and experiences contain these sparks. We have the power to redeem them and to return them to their divine origin by rescuing them from the *kelipot*, that is, by elevating the human experience to the level of the divine.

The elevation of the sparks is described as an act of *teshuva*: "What are the sparks in a sin? They are collectively the repentance

---

6. I. Baal Shem Tov, *Tzavaat HaRivash* (New York, 1975), p. 54.

for that sin. When you repent for a sin, you are elevating the sparks that were in that sin."[7] The Maggid of Mezeritch links the idea of *Tikkun* with our Sages' view that the process of *teshuva* can turn intentional sins into good deeds (Yoma 86b). He even claims that a sinful act contains holy sparks that can be redeemed.[8]

We will discuss below the potential that the practical application of the concept of elevation of the sparks presents for the successful implementation of the *teshuva* process. It allows the positive sparks to illuminate our failed past, and grants us the opportunity to lead a happier life. We will see that personal growth depends to a great extent on our ability to interpret the inner parts of our ego in a way that will provide us with positive feelings about ourselves and about our lives.

ELEVATION OF ALIEN THOUGHTS

Hasidism makes strenuous efforts to provide Jews with alternative sources of meaningfulness in addition to the narrow intellectual world of Torah study. In Hasidism, a rich emotional life serves as a channel of communication between God and man: God reveals Himself to man through the thoughts He sends him, which are described as "garments and covers behind which the Holy One...conceals Himself."[9] The Besht emphasizes that it is forbidden to repress or expel alien thoughts or evil impulses. Instead these should be channeled toward the individual's divine service.

Certain hasidic groups did not accept the Besht's principle. The rationalist worldview of Chabad Hasidism, according to which one must banish – that is, repress – alien thoughts, is a case in

---

7. Ibid.
8. Dov Baer, Maggid of Mezeritch, *Maggid Devarav LeYaakov*, p. 38.
9. M. Buber, *Hasidism and the Modern Man* (New York, 1958), pp. 204–205.

point. Yet despite the fact that the Besht's position is not shared within the entire spectrum of Hasidism, it nevertheless serves us as a helpful model. The following parable, which is described in the Besht's writings, explains how one must confront the urge to commit adultery and how it is possible to transform that *yetzer hara* into a helpful tool in the worship of God:

> If you are praying with great enthusiasm, you must ensure that you control any alien thought...such as thoughts of adultery. If you have thoughts of adultery, you must bring those thoughts to their source, which is the love of God... and you must tell yourself that adultery is part of the world of love.... If you suddenly see a beautiful woman, you should ponder what is the source of her beauty. After all, if she were dead, she would not have such a lovely face.... Therefore you must conclude that her beauty comes to her from the power of God that is flourishing inside her.... The source of her beauty is the power of God. Therefore, you should ask yourself, "Why should I long for part of this divine beauty when I can embrace the source and the fundamental element of all worlds where all beauty is located?"[10]

The Besht then goes on to link human feelings to the story of the shattering of the vessels, in light of the Ari's account of the creation of the world:

> I must think about this thing...that I fear or that I love... and I must ask myself where this fear or love comes from. After all, everything stems from God. He has given us feelings of fear and love even regarding bad things, such as, for

---

10. I. Baal Shem Tov, *Tzavaat HaRivash*, pp. 28–31.

example, wild animals; or, it could be said that everything stems from those qualities that fell to earth when the vessels were shattered. Therefore...why should I fear a single spark?... I should instead tie it up with profound awe and love, and I should do the same with all those qualities that fell to earth when the vessels were shattered. I must remove from the thing I fear or love the divine spark and I must elevate it to its source...because this is what every soul must do: it must elevate and return to their source all the sparks that fell during the breaking of the vessels.[11]

The Besht relates the issue of undesirable thoughts to the Ari's lofty account of Creation. As a result, he cannot imagine that thoughts may be meaningless. In his view, thoughts are the revelation of a divine spark that we must return to its source. We must therefore interpret this spark in a worthwhile manner. This interpretation will subsequently enable us to channel these undesirable thoughts so that they may positively impact our spiritual needs. Rather than repelling these forbidden thoughts from our minds, the Besht recommends that we contract ourselves in order to make room for them.

Within a religious framework, this kind of interpretive practice – of superimposing a lofty meaning onto stray thoughts – enables individuals and societies to flourish. Yet this strategy can also apply outside a religious setting, far beyond the confines of Hasidism.

Anton Boisen compared mentally ill persons in Western society and in other cultures.[12] He came to the conclusion that

---

11. Ibid., p. 45.
12. A.T. Boisen, "The Genesis and Significance of Mystical Identification in Cases of Mental Disorder," *Psychiatry* 15 (1952): 287–296.

only in the West does the repression of forbidden thoughts cause mental disturbances. In his view, this testifies to the latency of the Christian doctrine of Original Sin which still pervades Western society: "In most of our cases, the basic evil is ... personal unworthiness due to the presence of unruly desires ... which can neither be controlled nor acknowledged for fear of condemnation by the significant persons in one's life. These forbidden desires ... behave like ill-digested food."[13]

If this is the case, irrational or forbidden thoughts are not mental illnesses in and of themselves. What causes mental disturbances is the difficulty in accepting the fact that all people have such thoughts or such experiences.

Consider a young man who believes he is the Messiah, or the clinical case described by Theodore R. Sarbin: an elderly, unmarried woman who began hearing voices after she was fired from her job.[14] The young man distracts his attention from failure by inventing a fictional representation of himself, whereas the older woman invents for herself an intimate voice that accompanies her wherever she goes in order to compensate for her loneliness. In Western terms, we would designate the first case as "delusion" and the second as "hallucination." Now let us try to make these two people aware of the emotional vacuum that is causing them to create the replacement which society considers symptomatic of a disease. As clinical experience shows, although making patients aware of the source of their distress might not help them deal with their original problem, this awareness does at least help them cast off the social label of a "sick" person. They understand that their problem is not an illness, but stems from emotional distress.

---

13. Ibid., p. 288.
14. T.R. Sarbin, "The Concept of Hallucination," *Journal of Personality* 35 (1967): 359–380.

Furthermore, they can replace the stigma of the mentally ill, and might even avoid hospitalization.

The spiritual interpretation that the Besht proposes can direct patients to follow a path of personal development instead of distracting their thoughts from their problems. It can elevate them to a new level where their experiences have a positive value. It can also grant them an identity to be proud of, instead of condemning them to suffer from excommunication through hospitalization. The Besht's method of dealing with "alien thoughts" might perhaps strike one as naïve, or bring to mind mainstream techniques used in psychotherapy, where patients are encouraged to "ventilate," or in other words, to express their emotions verbally to a therapist. However, the proposition that stray thoughts can be "returned" to their divine source inserts itself in a broader idea in the thought of the Besht, which enables individuals to manage and extract meaning out of difficult situations.

ASCENT THROUGH DESCENT

The Western view of manic depression sees the manic ascent as serving the depression that will inevitably follow. This notion of "descent through ascent" implies that the true state of an individual suffering from manic depression is the depression itself; the ecstasy preceding it may simply be an attempt to escape from reality. Oriental religions encourage public expressions of mania and even revere those who manifest such ecstatic states. By contrast, in the West, such spiritual elevation is regarded as an uncontrollable deviation from the normal state of mental health.

The perception of these mood swings as a kind of insanity only exists in Western culture. Many intercultural studies on the subject show that shamans and religious leaders in other societies display a positive attitude toward those abnormal and ecstatic states of mind which the West defines as manic depression or even schizophrenia.[15]

In non-Western cultures, "abnormal" people are not considered sick. Rather, they are seen as individuals who can serve those whose job it is to heal others. Mircea Eliade, who studied shamans, argues that most shamans come "from particular families in which nervous instability is hereditary."[16] However, their culture does not regard them as victims of their mood changes. Instead, it teaches them how to monitor and control both their "schizophrenic-manic" tendencies and their epileptic episodes: "It is not to the fact that he is subject to epileptic attacks that the Eskimo or Indonesian shaman, for example, owes his power and prestige; it is to the fact that he can control his epilepsy."[17]

However, simply pointing out that manic depression is a Western phenomenon does not help us understand this state of mind. Before we look at the hasidic alternative, we must ask how a diagnosis of manic depression explains the upward and downward swings that are part and parcel of the human condition. Is the phenomenon interpreted as manic depression or depressive mania? In other words, is depression a momentary respite from the drive toward happiness in life (the mania) or is mania an illusory escape from life's basic state of depression?

In the Orient, where shamanism is commonly practiced, ecstatic or even epileptic attacks are an integral part of

---

15. K.R. Pelletier and C. Garfield, *Consciousness East and West* (New York, 1976), p. 23. See also J. Silverman, "Shamans and Acute Schizophrenia," *American Anthropologist* 69 (1967): 21–31, and O. Schwartzman, *Rofeh Lavan, Eilim Sheḥorim: Refuat Nefesh Maaravit BaJungel Shel Afrika* (Tel Aviv, 5767 [2006–2007]; in Hebrew), which describes the clinical experiences of a physician working with African tribes.

16. M. Eliade, *Shamanism: Archaic Techniques of Ecstasy* (London, 1964), p. 25.

17. Ibid., p. 29.

life; however, in the West, they are defined as symptoms of illness. Even mild cases of mania are considered deviations from the normal state of mind, and in more acute cases, the mania is seen as a façade, an obviously illusory attempt at self-defense or escape. Thus, the recommended clinical course of action is always to be suspicious of inexplicable states of happiness, out of fear that they are only an escape from the otherwise natural state of depression. Consequently, because such attacks cannot be given a positive value, we focus our efforts on how to prevent the damage they will inevitably cause. An anticipated result of the repression of such feelings is unexpected or even uncontrollable outbursts. In Western society, the cultural shortage of states of ecstasy or spiritual elevation is compensated for by the consumption of substances that can artificially induce such states (namely, alcohol and drugs).

In contrast with the Western model of "descent through ascent," Hasidism promotes the idea of "ascent through descent" (*yerida letzorekh aliya*). Living in a Western culture, we recognize depression as an unavoidable fact of life. However, if we take hasidic sources as our inspiration, we can learn how to positively transform descent leading to depression. In accordance with the kabbalistic worldview in which the descent can serve the ascent that will follow it (in line with the principle of "ascent through descent"), the way to reverse the descent is by giving it spiritual meaning.[18]

In light of the above, we can understand Rabbi Jacob Joseph of Polonne's statement that "the main purpose of our having been created from substance and form is that we must

---

18. Another psychologist who used the assigning of meaning to key elements in personal life as a means of coping with difficult situations was Viktor Frankl; see V.E. Frankl, *The Doctor and the Soul* (Middlesex, 1965).

try every day of our lives to turn substance into form."[19] This hasidic thinker expects us to use the substance in our lives and to give it form, that is, to give it meaning. States of descent or meaninglessness are trials that face us constantly. Our challenge is not to alter the script of our lives, but to interpret that script in a meaningful way.

The Besht also tries to include painful experiences in the overall evaluation of a person's life-story. On the verse: "There was evening and there was morning, one day" (Gen. 1:5), he teaches that the word for evening, *erev*, alludes to *taarovet*, a mixture, and in reference to the Creation, a state of confusion or depression. In contrast, the word for morning, *boker*, alludes to *bikoret*, a state of clarity and control. These two states create one entire day.[20] Thus, the Besht depicts the state of depression and the manic state as two sides of the same coin that create a single life-unit: one day. In his opinion, the Divine Presence is to be found in painful experiences, and even in transgression:

God gave us the *yetzer hara* in order to test us, just as one tests an infant who is learning to walk. The *yetzer hara* creates difficulties for us and turns simple things into complicated affairs in order to lead us on a crooked path. If we are wise, we do not let the *yetzer hara* triumph over us and we thereby give God great pleasure, just like a well-behaved, diligent son who gives his father great pleasure when a guest tests the son, asking him difficult questions, and the son does not allow himself to be defeated.[21]

19. Jacob Joseph of Polonne, *Toldot Yaakov Yosef*, p. 341.
20. I. Baal Shem Tov, *Sefer HaBesht Al HaTorah* (Jerusalem, 1975), p. 47.
21. I. Baal Shem Tov, *Keter Shem Tov*, p. 37.

What transforms a painful and sinful experience into a positive episode is interpretation. In the parable, we are compared to the diligent son who undergoes negative experiences among "adults" – including God – whose hearts fill with affection as they observe him passing the various tests. These tests are so essential that the Besht even says, perhaps slightly tongue-in-cheek, that they act like an inoculation. On the verse in Ecclesiastes: "For there is not a righteous man upon earth, that doeth good, and sinneth not" (7:20), he comments: "If we do good without doing anything wrong, the *yetzer hara* tries to induce us to sin, but when the *yetzer hara* sees that we have a little of himself in us, it abandons us and that is that."[22] In other words, when the *yetzer hara* sees that our "commitment" to it has been fulfilled because we do not always act properly, it stops provoking us. In this way, a small dosage of *"yetzer hara* germs" strengthens the immune system against the illness of sin.

HASIDIC JOY

The hasidic concept of "ascent through descent" is not limited to interpreting sinful behavior. The Besht uses the phrase "running to and fro" (*ratzo vashov*) to describe highly emotional states of mind. This expression harkens back to Ezekiel's vision, in which angels, referred to as *ḥayot* (usually translated as "living creatures"), are seen running back and forth before God's Throne of Glory. The Besht likens the movement of these angels to that of men before God: "It is written: 'The *ḥayot* ran to and fro' (Ezek. 1:14). Human vitality [here the Besht uses a pun: instead of *ḥayot*, living creatures, he uses a word that sounds very similar, *ḥiyut*, vitality] is to be found in the secret of contraction and expansion."[23]

---

22. Ibid., p. 30.
23. I. Baal Shem Tov, *Sefer HaBesht Al HaTorah*, p. 63.

Hasidism clearly does not deny the existence of depression, but it adamantly refuses to consider depression and emotional restraint as healthy or desirable states of mind. Thus, the "depressing evening" (using the motif from the Creation; see above) becomes an essential respite, a moment of repose, before the "morning that illuminates and rouses," in which we awaken in joy and ecstasy:

> The meaning of this image of the living creatures (*ḥayot*) running to and fro is that we all yearn for, and passionately wish to adhere to, our origins in the upper world…. If we are always excited, we will be unable to maintain ourselves in the real world. Thus, God has arranged the world in such a way that sometimes we focus on our physical needs, such as eating and drinking…. During those times our souls rest and our mental power is strengthened so that the soul and mind can return to serving God afterward. This is what is meant by "The living creatures (*ḥayot*) ran to and fro."[24]

The meaningless, mundane events are intertwined with those containing great excitement, in a relationship which "connects the days of smallness with the days of greatness."[25] The Besht explains: "In order to understand what smallness and greatness are, consider a person who is studying Torah but who does not understand what he is studying; that is a moment of smallness. However, when that same person studies Torah, understands the text, and becomes excited about it, that is what is called being on the steps of greatness."[26] Experiences of great insight and meaning may arouse

---

24. I. Baal Shem Tov, *Keter Shem Tov*, p. 38.
25. I. Baal Shem Tov, *Sefer HaBesht Al HaTorah*, p. 64.
26. I. Baal Shem Tov, *Keter Shem Tov*, p. 44.

great excitement, while moments of minor significance, in which people act "only because they have to, and with great effort and no enjoyment," are here understood as moments of depression.[27] The experiences of greatness can serve to elevate our periods of smallness and incorporate them into a single, optimistic world-view. This also represents a suitable description of therapy, which consists of ordinary as well as turbulent, revelatory moments.

The entire image of the "living creatures [that] ran to and fro" (lit. "ran and returned") refers to those moments of greatness and ecstasy, to the "morning"; the reason is that "we all yearn for, and passionately wish to adhere to, our origins in the upper world." The call to utilize moments of depression as opportunities for repose enables us to incorporate such moments in the story of our spiritual aspirations. The descent is a contraction of the ego and its ambitions. It is not an ideal situation when an individual's stature is lowered. We must remain alert during those fluctuations and maintain an awareness of our objectives: "From the power of those moments of smallness, we will move on to greatness – just like embers. If a single spark remains in the embers, the flame can grow and grow until it becomes the mighty bonfire it was in the beginning."[28]

The goal of "ascent through descent" is *devekut*, devotion to God. The Besht describes *devekut* as an intense, ecstatic state of mind that manifests itself in tremors and a high state of awareness, as if the person were disconnected from the world. Today, we might perhaps perceive the Besht's concept of ecstasy as psychotic behavior; his disciples, however, emphasize the potential of such ecstatic moments:

---

27. I. Baal Shem Tov, *Sefer HaBesht Al HaTorah*, p. 63.
28. I. Baal Shem Tov, *Keter Shem Tov*, p. 48.

During the repetition out loud [that is, the cantor's repetition] of the *Shemoneh Esrei* prayer, the Besht's tremors were very strong, as they always were whenever he prayed. Those who observed the Besht in prayer noticed how his body would shake as he recited those prayers. When one of his disciples, Reb Wolf (Zev) Kitzes, gazed at the Besht's countenance, he saw that the Besht's face was glowing with the power of several torches and that his eyes were bulging from their sockets. They were open and motionless, like those of a dying person, Heaven perish the thought. Reb Zev motioned to Reb Avraham and the two of them supported the Besht, bringing him to the cantor's podium. He walked together with them and stood before the podium. After his body shook violently for a few moments, he began the *Hallel* prayer, his body continuing to shake. Afterward, when he had finished saying the *Kaddish* prayer, he stood and continued to shake for a very long while. The reading of the Torah scroll was delayed until he stopped shaking. However, I also heard from the rabbi of the holy community of Polonne…one day he saw that, as the Besht prayed, the water in a large vessel moved around, the Divine Presence hovered above the Besht, and the earth therefore shook.[29]

Although *devekut* involves a temporary severance of ties with reality on the part of the worshipper, which can help alleviate tensions, it can also impact reality itself. Rabbi Nachman of Bratslav, the Besht's great-grandson, shows how, from a state of *devekut*, it is possible to retroactively elevate a state of depression:

---

29. S.A. Horodetsky, ed., *Sefer Shivḥei HaBaal Shem Tov* (Tel Aviv, 5735 [1974–1975]), p. 103.

One day, Rabbi Nachman began to study Torah, focusing on the literal meaning of the verses. Sometimes, he felt like a very simple man and, during this study of the literal meaning of the text, he would revive his spirits by recalling the journey he had made previously to the Holy Land. He explained the matter... and said... that he did not know anything at that moment; afterward, he said that he was afraid... then he said that he was very happy about having journeyed to the Holy Land.... He was extremely happy and scolded Reb Naftali for being too shy to play a tune.... He was in great spirits.[30]

Rabbi Nachman directs his attention to his own depression. He overcomes it by associating the experience with his journey to the Holy Land and reaches an exalted state of mind, which he then tries to impart to those around him. In Rabbi Nachman's philosophy, one can find many ways to elevate oneself from a state of "smallness," and to turn sorrow into joy. Rabbi Nachman envisions a technique of "nonsense" to raise one's emotional state or to distract one's thoughts constructively:

Here are a few ways to make yourself feel happy at all times.... Generally speaking, you can make yourself feel happy by uttering nonsensical words that make you laugh and by telling jokes to yourself... because depression (*mara shehora*) and sadness can overcome a person more than anything else. It is hard to overcome this sadness, which can be very harmful to you.[31]

---

30. Nachman of Bratslav, *Hayei Moharan*, p. 85.
31. Ibid., p. 72.

Instead of suggesting that we impose meaning and discipline on ourselves when all meaning has been lost, Rabbi Nachman advises us to fight the depression (which he refers to as *mara sheḥora*, black gall) by celebrating meaninglessness, with silly statements and jokes, in order to place the experience in its right perspective.

In hasidic terminology, the concept of "ascent through descent" works alongside the notion of *madrega*, meaning "level" or "step." Like a steel spring that has been compressed, every difficult situation into which we contract ourselves elevates us to a higher *madrega*, as the Besht says: "It is written, 'The living creatures (*ḥayot*) ran to and fro,' because we all passionately want to return to our origins.... The soul takes a respite from its enthusiasm and afterward returns with even greater devotion."[32] The Maggid, too, emphasizes that the "descent is needed for the ascent in order to reach a higher *madrega*."[33] The descent for the sake of ascent is important both for the sake of personal growth, and also because it gives us pleasure, as Rabbi Jacob Joseph of Polonne explains: "The reason we do not always remain on the same *madrega* is that continual pleasure is not real pleasure. Thus, sometimes we descend so that, when we ascend, we will derive even greater pleasure."[34] We see, therefore, that *rehabilitation* from a depressed state is not sufficient; *progress* to a point hitherto unattained, or what I call "pro-rehabilitation," is also required.

The ascension of *madregot* is not exclusively an individual matter. The tzaddik who ascends prompts those around him to

---

32. I. Baal Shem Tov, *Keter Shem Tov*, p. 10.
33. G. Scholem, *Devarim BeEgo* (Tel Aviv, 1976), p. 344.
34. E. Steinman, *Shaar HaḤasidut* (Tel Aviv, 1957), p. 83.

climb with him.[35] Rabbi Jacob Joseph sees the elevation of the entire community as the goal of the tzaddik's ascent:

> Even when devoutly religious Jews reach one of the higher *madregot*, they cannot stand on one *madrega* for very long.... He ascends so that those who are less worthy than him can also ascend the *madregot*.... Sometimes his head touches heaven as he ascends the upper *madregot*.... In any event, no matter which *madrega* the tzaddik is standing on, "God is stationed above him" to protect him from sin as he descends in order to be together with the masses; God protects the tzaddik when he descends so that the tzaddik will not learn from the sinful ways of the masses.[36]

In Hasidism, one of the simplest and most common ways of elevating the community spiritually is through joyful, communal celebrations. The tzaddik brings joy and happiness to others, which in turn gladdens his own heart, as in the following parable by Rabbi Jacob Joseph:

> This idea can be understood through the following parable: A prince was in the company of villagers when he received a letter from his father. He wanted to rejoice; however, he was embarrassed to show his joy in front of the villagers and was even a little afraid of them. What did he do? He ordered that they be given alcohol so that they could rejoice together with him and so that he could rejoice over his father's letter.[37]

---

35. On this point, one can cite as an example Rabbi Shlomo Carlebach's ecstatic performances among groups of alienated youth.
36. Jacob Joseph of Polonne, *Toldot Yaakov Yosef*, p. 81.
37. Ibid., p. 451.

The meaning of the parable is clear: The tzaddik (the prince) rejoices when he receives a divine message; however, he does not want to rejoice alone. Therefore, he makes those around him happy by giving them wine and enabling them to share in his spiritual joy.

THERAPY, THE HASIDIC WAY

Psychotherapy focuses solely on the past: the Freudian therapist sits on the couch, while his patient engages in an Oedipal struggle by watching again and again the film of his past until he can fight and defeat it: he looks the past straight in the eye, kills it, and grows from having defeated it.

The source of this retrospective viewpoint is Christianity, which believes that a person must acknowledge his share in the Original Sin in order to achieve salvation. In Catholicism, this is achieved through deep remorse and confession before a priest; in Protestantism, it is done through the individual's constant battle with his conscience or through accepting that he cannot know whether he has been predestined as one of God's elected. In psychoanalysis, the retrospective viewpoint takes the form of a continual search for some dark, formative event that can explain the patient's present difficulties. The search is often accompanied by despair, which becomes part of the motivation for this journey of delving into the patient's past.

In contrast to this "retrospective therapy," Hasidism offers "prospective therapy," which is oriented toward the future, unlike psychoanalysis, which focuses on the past. The psychology of Tzimtzum opens up the possibility of change, of *teshuva*, by teaching us to adjust our attitude toward our past. Hasidism sees no need to defeat the past; rather it instructs us to use the past to lead us to a genuine *teshuva*. The verbal root of the word *teshuva* – SH-V-B, to return – indicates it is a return to a starting point. We contemplate and reinterpret our past in a way that will prompt us to change our behavior in a positive way in the future.

"Three instructions that arouse the mind have been transmitted by Hasidism," writes Rivka Schatz-Uffenheimer. "Never despair, never let yourself become sad, and never have regret."[38] Hasidim avoid contemplating their past because, according to their leaders, doing so has no positive purpose with regard to the future: it creates an unhealthy obsession over previous transgressions and prevents us from being concerned with *Tikkun*. For those trying to undergo a process of change, the image of the inescapable past presents all the features of the tyrannical father, whom we discussed in the previous chapter.

This approach is not confined to the theoretical sphere in Hasidism. In hasidic communities, it is translated into a comprehensive program that the communal leader carefully imparts to his followers. Take, for example, the sermon delivered on the eve of Yom Kippur by the Rebbe of Gur, as cited by Martin Buber:

> The present, this "now," which is the moment during which we are speaking, did not exist when the world was created and will also never return. The present "now" was preceded by another "now" and will be followed by another "now." Each "now" has its own unique divine task .... Those who constantly think about the sins they have committed, about the evil acts they have done, are involved in those thoughts because we immerse ourselves in whatever we are thinking. Their entire soul is immersed in those thoughts and these people are therefore immersed in evil. If they are in such a situation,

---

38. R. Schatz-Uffenheimer, *ḤaḤasidut KeMistika: Yesodot Kviyetistiim BaMaḥshava HaḤasidit BaMe'a HaShmoneh Esrei* (Jerusalem, 5728 [1967–1968]), pp. 41–54.

they are incapable of returning to the righteous path.... Furthermore, there is also the danger that these thoughts might lead them to sadness.... It does not matter whether you push aside the mud this way or that way, it is still mud. "Did I sin or didn't I sin?" What possible benefit does Heaven derive when I keep on asking myself such a question? After all, I could instead spend my time creating beautiful necklaces that will bring joy to Heaven. As it is written, "Depart from evil and do good" (Ps. 34:15 and 37:27): do not dwell on evil; instead, do good things. If you have done something wrong, then compensate for it by doing something good.[39]

The Rebbe of Gur has harsh words for those who contemplate their past and, as a result, engage in self-recrimination. When we drown ourselves in thoughts about past transgressions, we cannot change. This is the fundamental difference between the Christian attitude, which focuses on regret over the past, and the approach of halakha, which concentrates on self-improvement. In identifying the roots of his condition in his past, a patient might also identify with that past. This would represent a major drawback in retrospective therapy, since it thwarts his efforts to change. The diagnosis therefore turns the "illness" into an irreversible condition, or a self-fulfilling prophecy. The patient may sink, as a result, into depression, and further undermine his chances of recovery. The Besht even goes so far as to describe the retrospective viewpoint as a representative of the *yetzer hara*:

> Sometimes the *yetzer hara* misleads us and tells us that we have committed a major sin when it was only a minor one or perhaps not even a sin at all. The *yetzer hara* does so because

---

39. M. Buber, *Or HaGanuz*, pp. 457–458.

all it wants to do is to make us feel depressed…. We must understand this deceitfulness and we must say to the *yetzer hara*, "I am going to ignore your fastidiousness and your claim that I committed a major sin, because all you want to do is to make me feel sad. Moreover, I will serve God with joy…." Even if he makes a mistake and transgresses, God forbid, he will not allow himself to become overly sad…. Instead, he will continue to serve God with gladness.[40]

The Besht's approach could prove beneficial for those who are trying to undergo a therapeutic process in an effort to change. He identifies the potential danger of delving too deeply into the past and is prepared to forgo needless "soul-searching" that can cause a person to sink into profound sadness. In light of the Besht's harsh criticism of "retrospective therapy," I wish to put forward another non-judgmental and compassionate way of looking at the past. In fact, what I am proposing is a reinterpretation of the past. People who reinterpret their past create a new autobiography, write a new musical composition of their life, and produce a new life melody. This reinterpretation of their autobiography, known as "biographical recomposition," constitutes a positive return to the past and contains the possibility of change in the future.

We find an example of biographical recomposition in the meeting between Joseph and his brothers in the Book of Genesis. The brothers are racked with guilt after having sold Joseph into bondage. These guilt feelings emerge in moments of crisis: "They said one to another: 'We are verily guilty concerning our brother, in that we saw the distress of his soul, when he besought us, and we would not hear; therefore is this distress come upon us'" (Gen. 42:21). When he reveals himself to his brothers, Joseph sees

---

40. I. Baal Shem Tov, *Tzavaat HaRivash*, pp. 14–15.

that their anxiety over the past stands between them and himself; he therefore beseeches them: "And now be not grieved, nor angry with yourselves, that ye sold me hither; for God did send me before you to preserve life" (45:5). Joseph reinterprets their evil act, by stressing its positive outcome. Adopting the omniscient perspective of God, he explains that he arrived in Egypt in order to rescue his family and the Egyptians from starvation. By selling him into bondage, the brothers were in fact performing an act of God: "So now it was not you that sent me hither, but God; and He hath made me a father to Pharaoh, and lord of all his house, and ruler over all the land of Egypt" (45:8). Joseph views his sale into slavery with hindsight, and thereby casts off the guilt associated with the act. He rewrites the story, and gives it a happy ending which inspires change. Similarly, when Joseph suggests storing the surplus of wheat harvested during the years of plenty in order to feed the Egyptians during the famine, he is using Pharaoh's dream as raw material subject to change, rather than as an irrevocable decree. Guilt feelings only lead people to dead ends; his point of view, in contrast, is forward-looking and positive.

In the previous chapter, we described the danger of a diagnosis that excludes the patient from society, and compared psychological diagnosis with the interpretation of ancient texts. In reinterpreting our past, we too can choose a strategy suitable to the process of change we wish to go through. The Besht teaches us that we must not surrender to the tyranny of the past, that we must open ourselves up to new ways of interpreting it.

In my view, orthodox Freudian interpretation is similar to Karaism, where a person interprets the past in accordance with a single, unique, and binding interpretation.[41] Freud envisioned

---

41. For an extensive discussion of this point, see my book: M. Rotenberg, *Rewriting the Self*.

a treatment that would subjugate the patient's entire stream of associations to an interpretation of a complex rooted in the individual's childhood. Instead of this static interpretive methodology, I suggest biographical recomposition as a technique inspired by the exegetical approach of midrash. When the midrashic mind reflects upon the biblical text, it does not seek to convey a predetermined, unique truth, but rather opens itself up to various interpretations, and chooses the most effective one among them. In the world of midrash, there is more than one "correct" or "original" interpretation. Midrash is founded on a perception of truth that allows for the existence of an entire range of interpretations that can coexist and which do not necessarily contradict one another.

There are midrashim which reflect on biblical figures who acted sinfully, and interpret their actions in a creative manner so as to "acquit" them. The most famous among these midrashim is the talmudic debate over David's sin (regarding Bathsheba): R. Shmuel b. Naḥmani cites R. Yonatan, who stated: "Whoever says that David sinned is mistaken" (Shabbat 56a). The midrash describes for us a complex legal situation that results in Bathsheba receiving a divorce decree (*get*) from her husband Uriah before the alleged sin was committed. David's testimony concerning himself, "I have sinned against the Lord" (II Sam. 12:13) is interpreted by the Talmud as merely a procedural sin. The Talmud applies the same approach to other biblical figures, each time exonerating them from their sins.[42]

This recomposition is a process that, in traditional terms is referred to as *teshuva*, repentance, the personal rehabilitation of a sinful past. In the process of recomposition, an individual's past is reinterpreted; the simplistic interpretation of that past contracts itself to make room for an alternative one which mitigates the sin

---

42. Ibid., pp. 75–85.

that is too onerous to bear. This process creates a change in the perception of the past, expressed in the revolutionary declaration of Resh Lakish: "*Teshuva* is so great an event that it converts maliciously committed sins into good deeds" (Yoma 86b). Resh Lakish is not referring to a past that is erased and thus vanishes, but rather one that is open to dialogue and changes according to its relationship with the present. It is a past that changes for the good and becomes good in itself, a story that is granted a happy ending.

Biographical recomposition empowers us to hear a new melody in our lives that generates positive change. This change is inevitable when our interpretation is open and committed to growth. Psychoanalysis has remained so committed to the Oedipus story that it is incapable of prompting change. We have many stories about hasidic leaders who, on hearing of people who deviated from the accepted norm, refused to pass judgment on them and recomposed the life stories of these "sinners" in a manner that gave them the benefit of the doubt and drew out the best in them. Let us present here, as an example, the story of the Seer of Lublin, from Martin Buber's *Or HaGanuz*:

> A man who committed major sins lived in Lublin. Whenever he asked to speak with the Rebbe, that tzaddik would accede to his request and would converse with him in the same way the Rebbe conversed with his closest, most loyal followers. Many of the Rebbe's followers were angry over this state of affairs, and one of them said to his friend, "The Rebbe knows every detail of a person's life from the first moment they meet and can read on a person's forehead all the reincarnations of that person's soul. Then how is it possible that the Rebbe cannot see this man is a sinner? And if he sees that the man is a sinner, why does the Rebbe have

anything to do with him and why does the Rebbe honor the man so much by conducting long conversations with him?" The two followers finally mustered the courage to ask the Rebbe these questions. He replied, "Of course, I know about him, just as you do. However, you both know how much I love to be happy and hate to be sad. This man is such a big sinner. Other sinners at least feel remorse for a moment. After they have sinned, they are sorry for a moment and then they go back to their evil ways. Well, this man feels no sorrow and never harbors a sad thought. He lives inside his happiness as if it were a tower and the light of that happiness has captivated my heart."[43]

The Seer of Lublin does not deny the negative value of a sin. Quite the contrary, he holds the sinner in great esteem on account of his sins. The Seer finds in sins that are committed with no pangs of conscience a simple joy that "captivates his heart." With a humorous note in his voice, he assigns the quality of joy to a sin that is committed without contrition.[44] In this way, the Seer views that man's life from another perspective, one that promotes constructive thinking. A social or therapeutic setting may therefore enable positive change.

In biographical recomposition, the past does not vanish: the details of the past remain in the patient's heart but are given a new melody that creates a healing continuity – or, in traditional Jewish terminology, *teshuva*. Whereas the dialectical approach is linear (the past must be abandoned for the sake of a better future), the concept of *teshuva* (to return) is cyclical: we cannot forsake

---

43. M. Buber, *Or HaGanuz*, pp. 268–269.

44. On humorous interpretation as a therapeutic tool, see my book: M. Rotenberg, *Rewriting the Self*.

our past in order to realize a better future; we must instead "return" to our past with a more positive mindset.

Biographical recomposition can, to a certain extent, be compared to narrative psychology. Narrative psychology, which has recently become quite popular, allows patients to create their own stories. There is, however, a substantive difference between both methods. Narrative psychology places patients at the center where they create their own, solipsistic narrative, and are not confronted with the need to self-contract. Biographical recomposition, in contrast, is only effective within a society that embraces the concept and enables people to compose new melodies for themselves. It requires a society, an audience to listen to and affirm the new melody. It does not allow the patient to dwell in his solipsistic narrative. It is like the joke of the Hasid who tells his wife that he had dreamed the previous night that he had become a hasidic leader. His wife responds: "Now all you need is for the other Hasidim in your group to have the same dream." In reality, hasidic rabbis acquired their leadership status only because their community assigned it to them. A narrative-oriented interpretation must find a community that will listen to it; it cannot operate within a vacuum. An interpretation that is stranded in a vacuum creates an unlimited range of interpretations, which turns the entire process of interpretation into an absurdity. Biographical recomposition succeeds when the audience takes pleasure in new melody. Elsewhere I have suggested that the process of mourning is an illustration of biographical recomposition, where the deceased's friends talk about him in the presence of the grieving family, creating a new life story in which the loss of a loved one is integrated into a positive context.[45]

---

45. See my book: M. Rotenberg, *Shekhol VeHaAggada HaHaya: Lo HaMaaseh Ikar Ella HaMaasiya* (Tel Aviv, 2005).

In a comparative study I conducted on the rehabilitation of former prisoners in kibbutzim versus the rehabilitation of prisoners in yeshivas, I showed how a traditional Jewish society can encourage its members to recompose their lives to the tune of a new melody and enable that melody to be accepted by the general community.[46] Both the kibbutz and the yeshiva are complete social environments that provide rehabilitees with a new frame of reference grounded in a new set of values. In the interviews that we conducted, we examined the rehabilitees' attitudes toward their past. Among those who were undergoing a rehabilitation process in a kibbutz, we noted a very prominent desire to "turn over a new leaf," to be reborn. They perceived the relationship between past and present in terms of conflict, and the past was regarded as a threat: "In order to rehabilitate yourself, you must forget your past, you must sever your ties with the past" or "I love life on the kibbutz but I am always afraid that people will accuse me of something that I did in my past; that would just destroy my present."

Among former prison inmates undergoing rehabilitation in a yeshiva, there was a great need to tell their story as a narrative that included their past: "I don't have to forget my past...you can make lemonade from a lemon, after all...I was in a situation that could be described as 'descent for the sake of ascent.'" The rehabilitee cited here used this hasidic phrase as a therapeutic tool which played a pivotal role in granting him a better present: "If I had not served my time in prison, I would never have been able to understand the truth." Another interviewee wanted to preserve the memory of his past because it enabled him to tell his story as a *baal teshuva*, a penitent. The *baal teshuva* status carries a positive social label, a label of success:

---

46. Ibid., pp. 200–205. The citations from the interviews appearing below also appear in that book.

I want to recall that period in my life so that I can remember where I came from and where I have managed to bring myself to – I came from rock-bottom and have succeeded in reaching the peak of the mountain. I don't want to erase my past. My past helps me today to understand what life is all about – no one can play me for a fool now! My past helps me look at things in the proper manner, to know when someone means serious business or not. I am not a new person and life fills me with happiness.... I am so happy because today I know what my purpose in life is. I was a subhuman and that is why I will never look down on anyone; you see, I myself was in the gutter just like that other person might be now. That is my greatest joy.

This interviewee exemplified several levels of Tzimtzum with regard to the change he underwent. He did not reject his past, and he contracted himself in order to integrate his unpleasant past within his life story. Moreover, that past enabled him to contract himself toward others: he could avoid arrogance because he did not present himself as a perfect human being.

The process that enables us to change should not negate the dry facts of our lives, just as a midrash does not negate the literal interpretation of a biblical passage. It is interesting to note the words of Rabbi Judah Loew, the Maharal of Prague, on this very point:

We must never uproot [i.e. lose sight of] the *peshat* (literal meaning). It remains intact, while the midrash or *derash*, the allegorical interpretation, probes the depths of the text. Let me cite a parable to explain this point. The roots of a tree are deeply embedded in the ground, while the tree produces branches, fruit, and leaves. Everything emanates from those roots. The *peshat* constitutes the root of the text, which expands and expands, sprouting branches in every direction.[47]

The Maharal's metaphor is similar to the one by Hegel cited in the introduction of this book. Hegel conceives of a conflict: the flower negates the bud and the fruit negates the flower. In contrast, the Maharal brilliantly interprets the word *peshat*, the literal meaning of the biblical text, in association with *Hitpashtut*, "expansion" (both words share a common verbal root, P-SH-T, which connotes simplicity). According to the Maharal's metaphor, the tree expands into branches and fruit, all of which stem from the same root. Hence the apparent contradiction between the literal and non-literal interpretations does not generate a tension between them in representing the truth; they coexist peacefully and enrich our lives.

---

47. A. Kariv, *Kitvei Maharal MiPrag* (Jerusalem, 5720 [1959–1960]), vol. 2, p. 283.

Chapter 4

Issachar and Zebulun: The Interpersonal Dimension of Tzimtzum

In the previous chapter, we discussed the implications of the theory of Tzimtzum at the intrapersonal level. This chapter will focus on the theory of Tzimtzum in a society whose members contract themselves in relation to their fellow and neighbor. We will also touch on non-normative behavior within a given society, and how that society may deal with those who do not behave in accordance with its expectations.

The close relationship between two of Jacob's sons, Issachar and Zebulun, harkens back to Jacob's blessing to his sons on his deathbed, and Moses' blessing in his final address to the Israelites in the Book of Deuteronomy. Jacob blesses Zebulun and Issachar with the words: "Zebulun shall dwell at the shore of the sea, and he shall be a shore for ships, and his flank shall be upon Zidon. Issachar is a large-boned ass, couching down between the sheep-folds. For he saw a resting-place that it was good, and the land that it was pleasant; and he bowed his shoulder to bear, and became a servant under task-work" (Gen. 49:13–15). Moses blesses the tribes of Zebulun and Issachar as follows: "Rejoice, Zebulun, in thy going out, and, Issachar, in thy tents" (Deut. 33:18).

Our Sages understood the reference to Zebulun dwelling by the sea as meaning that this tribe engaged in commerce, while the allusion to Issachar's tent implied that Issachar toiled under the yoke of Torah. On the basis of this interpretation, the story of a symbiotic relationship between the two tribes took shape: Zebulun earned a living through commerce, and offered financial support to allow the tribe of Issachar to dedicate its time to Torah study. This arrangement, however, was not confined to these two tribes alone; it accurately reflects the interdependence of Jewish communities in the Diaspora for centuries. In these communities, there were two main groups, each of which represented a different ideal of self-fulfillment: those who studied and those who earned their living through hard work in the material world. Successful people know how to contract themselves in order to make room for others whose lives are guided by different values.[1]

This outlook contrasts with dialectical ideology, which conceives of competitiveness as a necessity. In point of fact, it is primarily the Western world which is characterized by this competitive way of life. Studies comparing interpersonal communication in Japan and North America described the style of Japanese

---

1. See the survey of historian M. Beer, "Issachar and Zebulun," in: *Bar-Ilan Yearbook* (Ramat-Gan, 1968), pp. 167–180.

communication as displaying a calculated measure of vagueness and as consciously using an indirect, allusive language.[2] This kind of interpersonal communication discourages people from speaking in a straightforward way; it places quiet passivity above unrelenting assertiveness: "A child raised in a Japanese family learns not to call attention to himself by being loud, conceited, or self-centered. Children who take verbal initiatives are generally not rewarded."[3] Thus, Japanese society frowns upon children who act haughtily or who talk too much in class, and relates sympathetically to those children whose feelings have been hurt, or whose self-esteem has suffered from such behavior on the part of others. In Japan, this form of humility is accepted etiquette among people of the same social status.

Western ideology, on the other hand, with its religious roots in Protestantism, expects people to fight for their rights and to be assertive, sometimes even aggressive. We must ask ourselves, however, what price we are paying for this perception of life as a continual struggle. We are made to believe that, if we are not assertive and do not stand up for our rights, we will be lowering our own self-esteem while other people will regard us with contempt. This value judgment makes it difficult to establish interpersonal relationships based on a non-combative attitude.

In a society that accepts this model, all social relationships are built upon the image of the authoritarian person who asserts his rights, regardless of the other person. This kind of image

---

2.   D. Haring, ed., *Personal Character and Cultural Milieu* (New York, 1956); C. Nakane, *Japanese Society* (Berkeley, 1970); C.L. Johnson and F.A. Johnson, "Interaction Rules and Ethnicity," *Social Forces* 54 (1973): 452–466.

3.   C.L. Johnson and F.A. Johnson, "Interaction Rules and Ethnicity," p. 457.

can be destructive for relationships such as marriage, which are dependent on cooperation. The self-improvement books designed to make a person more assertive frown on any kind of dependence upon others, on the grounds that it undermines independence.

The most obvious price that society pays for the image of the narcissistic "self-made man" is the damage to interpersonal relationships. The relationships that the self-made man establishes are created in his own image, that of a struggle for his rights, which carries no potential for teamwork. How can this man find happiness when his sole ambition is to derive fulfillment from overcoming the other person? Today's economic world illustrates this problem: it creates value systems that encourage all the players in the economic game to compete with one another for resources. Yet can a rich man really enjoy his wealth if only he reaps the benefit of the resources he has accumulated in the course of years of competitiveness? Can he create meaningful human relationships with those very same people who have been his rivals and whom he defeated in the battle for affluence?

Although Western culture does show considerable respect for altruism, such models of kindness are constantly undermined by the argument that people only give because they want to fulfill their personal need for giving. Giving that concentrates on the giver places him in a fundamentally egocentric system, which respects individuals who seek to fulfill themselves. In this particular case, this self-fulfillment is derived from the realization of a religious or an ideological imperative rather than the satisfaction of a hedonistic appetite. Whichever way we look at his benevolence, the giver remains in the center.

Returning to Issachar and Zebulun, let us see how S.Y. Agnon depicts their relationship and what happens when the two brothers meet in the World to Come:

When Issachar arrived in Gan Eden to receive his heavenly reward, they examined his book and found it written: Issachar occupied himself with the Torah for a total of two days. Issachar was astounded. He said, "Is it possible that I, who all my life never budged from the diligent study of Torah, and always accepted all the burdens of Torah learning – I am to be rewarded for only two days of Torah study?" They said to him, "Issachar, how did you make a living in that world that you just came from?" He said to them, "I had a brother named Zebulun, and he and I were partners. He lived by the sea and he went out on commercial ships. Since he earned enough for both of us, I sat and studied while he was working." They said to him, "If so, then all the Torah you studied is accounted to Zebulun's credit, because if not for Zebulun's work, you would not have been able to learn Torah. And therefore, you have already used up your heavenly reward by enjoying the delights of Torah on earth below."

Issachar heaved such a great sigh that his voice was heard throughout Gan Eden. Zebulun said, "That voice sounds like the voice of my brother Issachar." He went and found him in great straits. Zebulun turned to the heavenly court: "Isn't it true that whatever reward I received comes to me only because of my brother, Issachar, who was always busy with the study of Torah? The truth is that it is not I who sustained Issachar but Issachar who sustained me! And on top of that, now I should take away his portion in heaven also? God forbid that one of my father's sons should do that! Rather, let Issachar take my place here in Gan Eden." Issachar said to him, "My dear brother, can you possibly think that I would take away your place in Gan Eden? That you should suffer while I enjoy myself here?" Zebulun answered him, "It's not my place but your place. Whatever good they are giving me here is only in reward for the Torah that you learned."

Zebulun refused to return to his place in Gan Eden because Issachar was so upset, and Issachar refused to occupy the place because of his affection for Zebulun. Then the Holy One, blessed be He, said, "Issachar and Zebulun, each of you keeps deferring to the other. Because of such love, I will enlarge your portion in Heaven." At that moment, Zebulun's place in heaven expanded so there was room for Issachar, too.[4]

In Agnon's account, God bases the formula for interpersonal relationships on Tzimtzum: "You have both contracted yourselves." Issachar and Zebulun are presented in his story as two brothers who are concerned for each other's place in heaven. Yet this description of this imagined scene in the World to Come reflects the brothers' relationship in this world as well: their ideals of self-fulfillment promote, rather than compete with, each other. This attitude is very different from the Western perspective. It is a well-known fact that the Catholic Church used to disregard business activities that did not support the Church, as is the manner in which the West, ever since the early days of Protestantism, has focused all its attention on economic enterprise and has even turned money into a value that can determine the worth of any human activity, whether material or spiritual.

How can Isaachar and Zebulun's respective approaches to self-fulfillment coexist? Simply because they are so different: one is based on Torah study, the other on commerce. There is no exchange of services between Issachar and Zebulun because

---

4. S.Y. Agnon, "Issachar and Zebulun," *Forevermore: Stories of the Old World and the New* (S.Y. Agnon Library at the Toby Press, forthcoming).

their respective activities cannot be measured in the same terms: the value of Torah study cannot be measured in economic terms. The two models of self-fulfillment therefore remain eternally distinct from one another. Since their endeavors have no common basis for comparison, Issachar and Zebulun do not compete, but instead make room for one another.

TZIMTZUM AS SELF-REDUCTION, NOT SELF-NEGATION

Hasidic society resembles its Japanese counterpart in the sense that it values solidarity rather than alienation between its members.[5] Let us examine traces of altercentric thinking, a notion that places the other person in the center with us, in hasidic society. Our challenge is to build the model of an altercentric rather than altruistic relationship. We have already seen that the altruistic model is egocentric; the altercentric model, conversely, places the other at the center. It does not demand that you disregard your own ego, but rather that you maintain dialogue with the other. There is the danger that the altruistic model might abandon me in my solitude, which will only increase in the face of the idealistic image that I have created for myself. In such a situation, the other is important for me only as a means to satisfy my marvelous altruism. By contrast, in the altercentric model, the other does not just serve my quest for self-fulfillment, but possesses his own intrinsic value: only in the presence of the other can I contract myself.

Let us return to the story of the Creation in order to understand the concept of altercentrism. Two seemingly contradictory kabbalistic terms, *Tzimtzum*, self-contraction, and *Hitpashtut*, self-expansion, describe the process that unfolds in the divine

---

5. T. Doi, *The Anatomy of Dependence* (Tokyo, 1969); S. Poll, *The Hasidic Community in Williamsburg* (New York, 1973).

light during the world's creation. God, as it were, contracts Himself in order to create space for the world. In this way, He generates the possibility of a meaningful other, who can receive what God is giving. Although this process is depicted as Tzimtzum, God can also expand Himself into the vacuum He has created in order to grant His abundant goodness. In the kind of giving that takes place in the wake of Tzimtzum, the recipient is not swallowed up inside the giver; both the giver and the recipient remain independent.

Kabbala does not regard this procedure as a one-time instance of Tzimtzum that creates a world where God acts kindly toward humans. Kabbala conceives of Creation as an endless process of Tzimtzum and *Hitpashtut,* through which God's abundant light is returned to Him, from where it emanates and illuminates the world. Gershom Scholem likened this twofold divine operation to a constant cosmic action of inhalation and exhalation, in which God contracts Himself in order to make room for and create the entity that will receive His expanding bounty.[6] However, as opposed to breathing, depicted here is a process of forming a meaningful Other, whose attachment to God establishes a relationship of mutual influence.

In Hasidism, the negation of the ego – or, as the Maggid of Mezeritch terms it, the "reduction of the ego," as we shall soon learn – became central to human behavior as well as interpersonal relations. This idea expresses itself in a pun on the Hebrew word "ego." In Hebrew, the word for "ego" is *ani,* which also means "I" and which consists of three letters: *aleph, nun, yod.* These three letters, but in a different order – *aleph, yod, nun* – constitute the word *ayin,* "nothing." This play on words has been the focus of many sermons. We must aspire to cancel our own ego, the *ani,* and render it null

---

6. G. Scholem, *Major Trends in Jewish Mysticism.*

and void, in order to rise to the level of "nothing," *ayin,* in relation to both God and other human beings. We might say we undergo an "anti-assertiveness training" course. In the process of nullifying ourselves, we become indifferent to our private needs; however, our self-nullification is actually the source of our new emotional power. This power is referred to in the Besht's comments on Hillel's famous saying: *Im ein ani li, mi li,* "If I do not believe in myself, who will believe in me?" (Avot 1:14):

> When we pray, we must divest ourselves of our physicality, as Hillel says: "*Im ein ani li...*" (when I divest myself of my physicality – that is, if I negate my physical self, my ego). When we pray, we must reach the point where we do not feel a part of this world; in other words, we must reach the level where we neither know nor feel whether we really exist in this world or not. When we reach that level, we certainly need not fear foreign thoughts because they cannot approach us if we have divested ourselves of this world. That is the meaning of the latter part of Hillel's saying: "*mi li*" – literally: "who will be for me?" – that is, who will approach me, what foreign thoughts can approach me?[7]

In the Besht's opinion, the un-egotistical state – "*ein ani li*" (I divest myself of my physicality) – can strengthen us more than our egotistic concern with ourselves, as expressed in the two words: *ani li,* literally: "I am for myself," or: "I am concerned with my physicality." He recommends self-negation as a way of connecting ourselves to different parts of our ego which appear in the form of challenging thoughts. Commenting on the word *me'ayin,* "where" (lit., "from where") in the verse, "But wisdom, where

---

7. I. Baal Shem Tov, *Tzavaat HaRivash,* p. 10.

(*me'ayin*) shall it be found?" (Job 28:12), the Maggid infers from the word *ayin*, which means "nothing" (but which, in this verse, is part of *me'ayin*), that entering a state of nothingness is the only way to attain wisdom: "When you think of yourself as if you were nothing and reduce yourself to a tiny entity, God also contracts His Divine Presence...and then you can surely attain wisdom."[8] However, the Maggid does not propose that we attain wisdom by totally negating our ego, but simply by reducing it. Through Tzimtzum, we can make room within ourselves to absorb understanding from external sources. This is a wisdom that aggressive and competitive people can never attain.

Similarly, Tzimtzum is considered an essential tool in establishing our social relationships. Tzimtzum reinforces our value as human beings, with respect to both God and society. When we contract ourselves, we are emulating God who contracted Himself in order to create the world. In this way, we fulfill our obligation to participate in the world's redemption, and in a way, its creation: our human activities influence the divine. By emulating God, we redeem the divine sparks that fell to the ground of the material world.[9]

The tzaddik, as a role model, is frequently referred to in hasidic literature as "nothing" or a "nonentity."[10] Nevertheless, the extreme level of humility and spirituality that he attains does not distance him from his community. Quite the contrary, the tzaddik is commanded to include in his spiritual world his encounters with others. Rabbi Jacob Joseph of Polonne says that we must feel God's presence even in the simple stories others tell us. He even

---

8. Dov Baer, Maggid of Mezeritch, *Maggid Devarav LeYaakov*, p. 86.
9. I. Baal Shem Tov, *Keter Shem Tov*, p. 31.
10. G. Nigal, ed., *Torot Baal HaToladot: Derashot Rabbi Yaakov Yosef MiPolonne, Lefi Nosei Yesod* (Jerusalem, 5734 [1973–1974], p. 40.

allows for the possibility of engaging in prayer while listening to someone else's small talk.[11]

In his anthropological study on the hasidic world, Jonathan Shatil quotes one of his interviewees, a Bratslav yeshiva student, who describes how the concept of Tzimtzum works in his social life:

> The Torah's commandments enable us to contract the fiery, divine bounty.... At the same time, they reduce and channel our egotistical tendencies and feelings.... For instance, if you stand out intellectually or have remarkable leadership ability, you will find that these gifts fill you with excessive pride and render you incapable of being down-to-earth with others. You must stop being so sophisticated and you must relate to others as people who are worthier than you .... Each day, we are commanded to talk with others; we cannot cut ourselves off from the community. In fact, in your constant efforts to improve yourself spiritually, you must engage in conversations with your friends and must be sensitive to what they have to say. By eliminating your feelings of excessive pride, and by striving always to be straightforward, you can open your heart to the distress of others and identify with them.[12]

SELF-FULFILLMENT IN SOCIETY

Every society has its own value system with which its members identify. In order to create a society based on dialogue, we must consider the way in which we treat others as well as the way in

---

11. See S.H. Dresner, *The Zaddik*, p. 188.
12. J. Shatil, *Kontzeptziyot HaEnergia HaNafshit BeTorot Ishiyot Psikhologiyot UVaTefisa HaKabbalit-Ḥasidit: Darkhei Mimusha BiYshivat Baalei Teshuva Shel Ḥasidei Bratslav* (PhD diss., Jerusalem, 1987), p. 153.

which we derive self-fulfillment. Let us analyze two different kinds of society: one that offers a single option for self-fulfillment (mono-labeling) and one that offers several (multi-labeling).

A competitive society where relationships are "I or Thou" offers only one model for self-fulfillment, resulting in contention and struggle. The intriguing question is: what happens to those who cannot meet the standards set by this model? Those who fail to measure up are liable to develop an inferiority complex *vis-à-vis* those who succeed in that society. For example, in a culture that uses money as an instrument for determining the value of any object or action, a financially indebted person feels guilty. A culture that assigns a monetary price to everything is one that sees everything in economic terms; thus, a shortage in funds is immediately interpreted as a lack of everything. Money becomes the central value and people who lack money are regarded as deficient: they lack *goods* and thus they are not *good*. People who have failed to fulfill themselves (financially) and who depend on the goodwill of the bank that lends them money are likely to develop feelings of guilt and failure over their inability to meet society's expectations. If you cannot pay your (financial) debt, you are liable to be labeled "guilty" by society. This is an existential state that goes beyond the concrete debt that is owed. Your creditor can humiliate you, oppress you, increase your feelings of guilt, and even virtually turn you into a slave.

The guilt that the poor feel toward the affluent produces alienation, not gratitude. Feelings of gratitude stemming from interdependence exist only in elite societies that segregate themselves from the masses. In a society that values only one kind of excellence, those who do not achieve that brand of excellence experience frustration, resentment, and hatred. Such feelings can easily produce non-normative behavior, which expresses itself in criminality or in the inability to function in, and merge with, society.

INSTITUTIONS OF EXILE FOR "MISFITS"

How does a democratic society, which encourages us to express our free will, react to those who fail to function within its framework? Such people present this free society with a paradox: the social ideal of freedom, imposed as it is upon us. The presence of people who are unable to be free obligates this society to confront the issue of dependence. Hence this understanding of freedom as a universal right and obligation justifies the ostracism of or indifference toward those elements who cannot uphold it.

The most logical solution is to exile non-normative people from this society, and send them to institutions that function precisely in the opposite way: prisons or treatment centers. Although ostensibly these institutions are supposed to prepare their inmates for an independent way of life, where the realization of individual liberty is the only normative option, they function as totalitarian frameworks in every respect. Heavily policed, they monitor, through their staff, every move that each inmate makes.

Research studies have shown that the inmates in these institutions generally have no inclination to be released back into free society. Quite the contrary, their prolonged monitoring in a closed institution (irrespective of its nature – correctional or therapeutic) causes them to develop a strong desire to remain under this constant supervision and to receive the institution's treatment services.[13] Such findings are not surprising because these institutions

---

13. S.P. Segal and U. Aviram, *The Mentally Ill in Community-Based Sheltered Care* (New York, 1978). See also the comments of the editors of the following collection of essays: E.R. Sennett and A.D. Sachson, eds., *Transitional Facilities in the Rehabilitation of the Emotionally Disturbed* (Manhattan, 1970). In the introduction to the collection, Sennett and Sachson acknowledge the particularly low rate of success in returning inmates of facilities for the rehabilitation of the emotionally disturbed to a normative way of life in the "outside" world (p. vi).

promote the inmates' dependence on others in the very heart of a society that champions an extreme form of freedom.

Apparently, the existence of a single model for self-fulfillment is closely linked to the free society's competitive character where those who fail to attain the goal of self-fulfillment are doomed to view themselves, and to be viewed by others, as "debtors" who must feel guilty for their situation. In the end, these "debtors" are exiled from the free society and from its normative way of life. This exile is structural in nature, and it is the outcome of the structure of a society where there is only one model for self-fulfillment. The treatment institutions in that society are therefore doomed to failure in their attempt to rehabilitate these "social misfits" and return them to normative society.

A competitive culture sees conflict as a lever for self-development. It declares: "Whatever is mine is mine and whatever is yours is yours" (Avot 5:14), which is essentially the principle of competitiveness. With such an attitude, our efforts to stand out among the crowd do create interpersonal relationships, but these relationships are conflictual. They result in alienation and solitude. In contrast, Hasidism preaches an approach that transforms our relationships with others: we must contract ourselves in order to achieve a higher level of spirituality and include others. Instead of conflict, we have dialogue.

REINTRODUCING ISSACHAR AND ZEBULUN

What of the society, such as the hasidic one, that offers several options for self-fulfillment? Hasidism does not exile or reject anyone. Every individual, both normative and non-normative, has a place in society. By focusing on the interpersonal dimension of Tzimtzum, Hasidism provides the opportunity for a relationship between "material people" and "spiritual people." The philosophical terms "material" and "form" helped Hasidism resuscitate the classical relationship between Issachar and Zebulun that operated in the Jewish world until the seventeenth century.

In the sixteenth and seventeenth centuries, Eastern European Jewry enjoyed an institutionalized form of autonomy. The Council of Four Lands (*Vaad Arba HaAratzot*) was the main organ representing the major Jewish communities in the eyes of the authorities. This was a social system that was under the joint control of rabbis and *parnassim* (affluent Jewish communal leaders). The Council of Four Lands maintained well-organized educational and social service networks, collected taxes, and enabled the peaceful coexistence of "Issacharites" (the scholars) and "Zebulunites" (the merchants and artisans). The violent uprising of Catholic farmers in 1648 under the leadership of Bogdan Chmielnicki (also known as *Pera'ot Taḥ veTat*, the Disturbances of the Hebrew calendar years 5408 and 5409, because of the many Jews who were murdered by Chmielnicki and his supporters) weakened the central Polish regime, and marked the beginning of the decline of Jewish communal autonomy.

In the wake of the disturbances, the primary goal of the Polish government, and of the Council of Four Lands, became the collection of taxes. One could now only attain leadership positions in the Council through bribery, and the rabbis lost their status as an independent class. In this era, only affluent Jews were appointed to the post of rabbi, which meant that the two classes –the *parnassim* and the rabbis – merged into a single class of wealthy rabbis who grew increasingly alienated from the Jewish masses.[14] Testimonies

---

14. In his autobiography, philosopher Solomon Maimon (1754–1800) describes how scholars took pains to wear special attire that would distinguish them from the masses. This distinction was maintained even within the family (S. Maimon, *Chayei Shlomo Maimon* [*Katuv Bidei Atzmo*], translated from the German by Y.L. Baruch [Tel Aviv, 5702 (1941–1942)]. On the attitude of

from that era frequently refer to rabbis who show signs of impatience and intolerance toward Jewish villagers.[15] Thus only one

---

the scholars to the masses, see the testimony of Rabbi Joseph Dubno, who is quoted in H.M. Rabinowicz, *The World of Hasidism* (London, 1970):

> The leaders live in luxury and splendor and do not fear the burden of taxes and other communal levies. They impose heavy burdens on others and lighten their own burdens. They take the lion's share of all honours and distinctions...and the congregation of God, the children of Abraham, Isaac, and Jacob, are crushed and humiliated, left naked and barefoot by heavy taxes. (p. 27)

15. Here is how historian S. Dubnow describes this period:

> The distance between "Torah-Jews" and "non-Torah Jews," between the learned and the masses, steadily increased. In accordance with the basic rabbinical assumption that "the study of Torah takes precedence over everything else" (*"Talmud Torah keneged kulam"*), the group consisting of the community's talmudic students was always the prestigious cadre, which was also very aggressive. All those who joined this group looked down on the masses, who acknowledged their low status in comparison with the learned members of the community. (S. Dubnow, *Toldot HaHasidut* [Tel Aviv, 1975], p. 22)

Dresner presents the impressive testimony of Joseph HaKohen, who lived in the eighteenth century; this testimony depicts in a nutshell the withdrawal of the rabbis' support for the public. HaKohen speaks of a very learned rabbi who was known for his great intellect and who studied Jewish religious law and the Tosafot in a precise, amazing manner. One day, as he was immersed in his study, a woman dressed in rags appeared before him and told him about her extremely difficult financial circumstances. The rabbi rebuked her for having disturbed his peace of mind and the woman left with a heavy heart.

Joseph HaKohen adds the rabbi's interpretation of this incident. According to HaKohen, the rabbi quoted the overriding principle that Torah study takes precedence over everything else. He was very busy at the time, studying a complex, complicated matter, and in only two days' time he was to deliver a sermon on that material. Suddenly this woman appeared and the rabbi asked whether it was at all proper that he should interrupt his studies in order to judge in a dispute she had with another person (S.H. Dresner, *The Zaddik* [New York, 1960], p. 30).

model of self-fulfillment remained, and a new single ruling class of affluent scholars emerged whose way of life was markedly different from that of the "common people" in the Jewish community. Indeed, the members of this class viewed the common people's way of life with contempt.

Hasidism succeeded in reviving the relationship between the "material" and the "spiritual," the traditional Issachar-Zebulun partnership, by instituting the payment of dues to the tzaddik. The Hasid no longer needed to become a student of a rabbi to enter his congregation and receive his protection; he could instead assist the tzaddik financially. The introduction of the title "Hasid" allowed every Jew to feel valued, even if they were neither talmudic scholars nor affluent members of their community.

Rabbi Jacob Joseph of Polonne, in his commentary on why God commands the Children of Israel to give half a shekel each, rather than a whole shekel coin (Ex. 30:11–16), describes the relationship between the different groups in society as body and soul:

> The intention [of this commandment] is to teach the Children of Israel to regard themselves as a single, unified nation. No Jew must regard himself as distinct from his fellow; rather, he is to see himself as half a person. Only when he is joined to another Jew is he whole. That is why each Jew must give half a shekel and not a whole shekel coin…. Similarly, each of us consists of a body and a soul. However, the soul must not be arrogant, declaring itself superior to the body and claiming that it is holy and that it was hewn from a holy place…. Nor must the body be arrogant, declaring itself superior to the soul because it provides it with physical sustenance…. Body and soul need each other just as a man and a woman are each only half a person [and need each other in order to become whole]. Similarly, talmudic

scholars and tzaddikim must not declare that they have no need for the masses just because they are the pillars of the Torah. Nor must the masses be arrogant, declaring that they have no need for the talmudic scholars because those scholars depend on the masses' financial support. At the individual and social levels, both the material and the spiritual are needed in order to create a whole person.[16]

Social harmony is achievable if a community supports two ideals for self-fulfillment: the Issachar model and the Zebulun model. This system of complementary values allows for different lifestyles to coexist, without proponents of one considering themselves inferior to defenders of another. In such a society, the interdependence between its members is not a problem to be surmounted but a proper and desirable social order.

The Baal Shem Tov's commentary on the verse: "In all thy ways acknowledge Him" (Prov. 3:6) considerably expands the range of self-fulfillment options beyond Issachar and Zebulun.[17] He raises the possibility that salvation may be attained in every situation. The Besht also seeks to prevent those who have failed to achieve self-fulfillment in accordance with their society's expectations from becoming "debtors" to those who have achieved success.

MUTUAL RESPONSIBILITY

"Mutual emulation" (see chapter two) – namely, a relationship in which we see ourselves in others and thereby assume responsibility for them, because there is something of us in them – also plays a crucial role in social cohesion. Rabbi Jacob Joseph of Polonne

---

16. Ibid., p. 243.
17. I. Baal Shem Tov, *Tzavaat HaRivash*, p. 17.

assumes that this sense of responsibility starts with the way we relate to others:

> When looking at the failures of their own generation, Hasidim must each assume responsibility for those failures.... When looking at the failures of the tzaddikim and the Hasidim of their own generation, the people of the world (that is, the masses) must assume responsibility for those failures and must decide to repent.... The leader of the generation and the common people must always give each other the benefit of the doubt. While the leader of the generation must repent so that the members of that generation will do the same, the people must repent so that the head of the generation will be rewarded by heaven.[18]

From this point of view, one does not take pride in the shortcomings of others. Rather, we learn from them. This standpoint promotes mutual acceptance and offsets rivalry; after all, we are all part of a single body. We can now view salvation as a social concern, rather than a private matter. Furthermore, we do not need to adjust ourselves to any preconceived model. Whichever path we choose leads us to an awareness of God. This constitutes, according to Hasidism, the greatest Jewish ideal: to find religious value and meaning in every lifestyle. The tzaddik plays a major role in the inclusion of sinners within the framework of normative society. Rabbi Jacob Joseph views this role as an interpretive one: the tzaddik is called upon to give everyone the benefit of the doubt, to discover the religious meaning that can bestow value upon each person's lifestyle. The tzaddik undertakes this

---

18. Jacob Joseph of Polonne, *Toldot Yaakov Yosef*, p. 335.

interpretive process through introspection, identifying the sinner within himself and himself within the sinner (mutual emulation). The difference in status between the tzaddik and the transgressor demands of the tzaddik that he make room inside of himself for the sinner.

The reverse is also true: against the backdrop of Europe's revolutionary heritage, it would have been natural to expect that a society would condemn the crimes committed by its leaders and seek to depose them. Rabbi Jacob Joseph, however, recommends another option: the sins of the leaders can be regarded as a reflection of the misdeeds of the public. The public should thus also engage in communal soul-searching.

As we saw in the second chapter, mutual emulation can serve as an alternative to diagnosis. In a society governed by a uniform worldview, each individual is assessed according to a predetermined ideal. This society will label as "abnormal" and exclude those whose behavior is incompatible with this model. However, in a society which acknowledges more than one path toward self-fulfillment, a person can adapt to any ideal without being rejected as a failure. In hasidic society, all models are interconnected; they represent a single body in which all the organs complement one another. Thus, in order for me to judge others, I must make room for them within myself because they are a part of me and I am a part of them. This judgmental process can never lead me to reject others, but instead forces me to accept them by considering them as part of myself. A society would not reject or expel the deviant when following this method. Indeed, the society, as well as the tzaddik, would focus their attention on him.

Society uses the criminal and the mentally ill in order to define morality and sanity respectively. In doing so, society defines the norm in opposition to deviancy. In mutual emulation, the deviation itself is employed to help the deviant. As we saw in the previous chapter, a person's sinfulness can be seen as a descent for the purpose of ascent and can be instrumental in the spiritual growth of both the deviant and society as a whole.

Ultimately, the reader should remember that, from a dialogic standpoint, the practical meaning of the principle that "All Jews are responsible for each other" is that both the positive and the negative aspects that I recognize in others are also part of myself. Just as the artist seeks a response from others to his creation (*yetzira*), the deviation from the norm that I detect in others serves to balance my own urges (*yetzer*).

Chapter 5

Seeing the Voices:
The Suprapersonal
Dimension of Tzimtzum

Western psychology focuses on the individual's material existence, and shows no interest in his or her spiritual life. Out of a rejection of mysticism, it reduces mystical experiences to mere "feelings." People who have "heard voices" or witness a mystical vision are labeled as insane and excluded from their communities. In distress, they consult a psychiatrist, who explains to them that their experiences are the expression of emotional complexes arising from the suppression of their sexuality.

This shift in the world's approach toward madness did not originate in clinical practice, but within the precincts of religion. Its roots can be traced back to the sixteenth century and the Protestant revolution. In his treatise on the principles of religion, John Calvin argues that some individuals are irremediably cursed in God's eyes. This deterministic belief gave way to a new, humiliating approach toward the insane – they became labeled as damned creatures.[1] Protestantism also promoted rationality as the sole moral compass and as proof that an individual has been chosen by God and will be redeemed. It emphasized rationalist materialism against mystical spirituality, and sought to delegitimize irrational mysticism on religious and human grounds.[2] To this day, the Western individual cannot consider spirituality as a source of self-fulfillment. For psychology, as a scientific discipline and cultural paradigm, Tzimtzum is therefore a major threat.

In this manner, psychology has managed to construct a barrier that separates it from irrational experiences, and to turn the dialogue between reason and madness into a dialectic in which reason always triumphs over madness. In chapter one, I proved that this dialectic was not only found in psychology. In the nineteenth century, the driving force behind the historical progress of the human spirit from irrationalism to rationalism was entirely perceived in dialectical terms. However, this very same barrier also stands in the way of psychology when it tries to help people function in the everyday world after they have had mystical experiences. This barrier blocks out all irrational episodes from entering the human consciousness, admitting only rational thoughts. Thus, the very same trend that gave rise to psychoanalysis, which seeks to raise the irrational subconscious to rational consciousness, also pushes the central human experiences of spirituality and mysticism into the subconscious.

---

1. I expanded this argument in my first book: M. Rotenberg, *Damnation and Deviance: The Protestant Ethic and the Spirit of Failure* (New York, 1978).
2. M. Weber, *HaEtika HaProtestantit VeRuach HaKapitalism.*

My attempt at creating a dialogic psychology that does not simply talk *about* madness, but which instead engages in a dialogue *with* it, must find a way to grapple with the irrational. Western psychology tends to disregard mystical experiences and seeks to cure individuals who have gone through such experiences. I prefer to regard them with respect and without any trace of suspicion. I consider mystical experiences in the same way they present themselves: as proofs of the existence of the supernatural that is within each individual. I seek to develop a rational psychology that does not try to overcome the irrational supernatural, but which instead contracts itself in the face of the supernatural, makes room for it, and concurrently, asks the supernatural to accommodate it.

In this final chapter, I will apply the notion of Tzimtzum to our understanding of mystical experiences. The balanced method I am proposing here is based on the foundations of Tzimtzum and dialogue, on a merging of spirit and matter, body and soul. I wish to bridge this gap with the help of the concept of PaRDeS, which underlies Jewish exegesis and offers a range of possible exegetical approaches.

PARDES

The acronym PaRDeS is derived from the Hebrew word *pardes*, orchard, which, in Persian and other Indo-European languages, denotes paradise. In early Jewish mysticism, *pardes* referred not only to the biblical paradise, the Garden of Eden, but also metaphorically to the worlds we can discover through mystical experiences and spiritual elevation. The thirteenth-century Jewish mystic Rabbi Moses de Leon, in his book *The Wise Soul*, was the first to use the term as an acronym for four possible interpretations of a text: *peshat* (literal meaning), *remez* (symbolic or allegorical reading of the text), *derash* (homiletical interpretation), and *sod* (mystical interpretation).

This notion of PaRDeS can easily be appropriated by therapists who seek to bridge the gap between the rational and the irrational, and create a dialogue between sanity and madness.

Cognitive therapy makes use of *peshat* and assumes that there are certain conscious beliefs that are the source of the patient's anxieties. Therapists engage in a discussion with their patients in order to help them understand the error that has led them to embrace beliefs that are causing them anxieties or other problems. The therapist tries to induce the patient to replace these beliefs with more rational and helpful ones.[3] Theorists emphasize the difference between this approach and that used in psychoanalysis:

> In contrast to psychoanalysis, cognitive therapy deals with what is immediately derivable from conscious experiences. The cognitive therapist does not look for hidden meanings in the patient's thoughts, whereas the psychoanalyst deals with them as symbolic transformations of unconscious fantasies.[4]

Cognitive therapists, by way of *peshat*, do not interpret their patients' words by searching their subconscious. Instead, they interpret those words literally and seek to help their patients process and analyze their own beliefs. In this way, therapists try to make their patients' feelings more positive and improve their lifestyles on a day-to-day basis. In order to achieve these goals, cognitive therapy helps patients identify the beliefs that are leading them toward an impasse or to anxiety-driven obsessive-compulsive

---

3. R.E. McMullin, *Handbook of Cognitive Therapy Techniques* (New York, 1986), p. v.
4. A.T. Beck, *Cognitive Therapy and Emotional Disorders* (New York, 1979), p. 316.

behavior. By offering the option of "partial treatment," such therapy only deals with rationality and does not consider the soul. By its very nature, cognitive therapy can only be of limited use for patients who are committed members of rationalist Western society, since they can determine their own emotions and beliefs and reach self-awareness through rational analysis.[5] Nevertheless, *peshat* is essential because it is the basis for a clear understanding of both text and soul.

At the other end of the PaRDeS spectrum are spiritual-mystical experiences that give meaning to life and help us escape from or overcome the hardships of our environment. Due to their negation of the material world, spiritual-mystical approaches to life cannot make a significant contribution to Western society where *meaning* is constructed on the foundations of materialism and rationalism. There is a wide gap between Western, rational *peshat* and the irrational *sod*. The purpose of this chapter is to find a way to welcome *sod* into the world of the normal and sane.

Between the rational *peshat* and the mystical *sod*, we find *remez* and *derash*. Both manifest themselves in the therapeutic practice of biographical recomposition that I described in chapter three. Biographical recomposition employs the individual's imaginative faculties to provide the patient with a better life. I do not refer here to the kind of *peshat* interpretation that only allows for one definition of the written word, nor am I speaking of a mystical world detached from real life. Just like midrash, which is based on a relatively free interpretation of the biblical text, our imagination possesses a considerable measure of freedom, or poetic license, even though its anchoring point is reality. Because of this relative autonomy, the midrashic imagination can serve as a link in the PaRDeS.

---

5.   R.E. McMullin, *Handbook of Cognitive Therapy Techniques*, p. xiii.

Midrash allows for a more open interpretation than *peshat* and *sod*, creating a "bridge" between these latter two extremes, which enables them to validate each other. Midrash does not demand sole ownership of interpretation. The homilist knows that "the literal interpretation of the biblical text always remains" – in other words, the literal and straightforward interpretation of the biblical text remains intact even after the intervention of the midrashic mind.

A parallel to midrash as an interpretive process coexisting with, but not negating, the literal interpretation of a biblical text, is the world of human imagination, which is a narrative world that coexists with reality, yet does not threaten it. Imagination supplants reality in patients when they are unable to maintain the imaginative sphere alongside the real world, and to enable a dialogue between them. But imagination also promotes what I have referred to in the past as the creation of a "living legend"[6] (rereading events in a way that will help a person move forward in his life), and always has roots in historical reality, unlike myth, which does not require such anchoring because it is entirely based on supernatural events. Dialogue with our imagination can be a creative tool permitting the construction of a new imaginative legend that provides meaning to a failed autobiography.

FOUR ENTERED THE ORCHARD

The Talmud relates:

> We have learned: Four individuals entered the orchard. They were Ben Azzai, Ben Zoma, Aḥer [Elisha b. Avuya], and R. Akiva... Ben Azzai took one look and died... Ben

---

6. See my book: M. Rotenberg, *Shekhol VeHaAggada HaḤaya.*

Zoma took one look and was injured [that is, went mad] ...
Aḥer "trimmed the bushes" [that is, became an apostate]....
R. Akiva emerged unscathed. (Ḥagiga 14b)

Tradition regards the "orchard" in the talmudic story as the world of the mystical *sod,* and does not link it to the concept of multiple interpretations that is attributed to Rabbi Moses de Leon under the acronym PaRDeS. Nevertheless, I would like to make that connection in order to illustrate how the PaRDeS "bridge" between the real and mystical worlds (*peshat* and *sod*) materializes in certain types of human reactions. I am not proposing any textual interpretation of the talmudic passage; rather, I am presenting an analysis of different kinds of behavior. I believe that the responses of these four individuals reflect four separate reactions to the world of *sod.*

Of the four individuals in the story, only one of them – R. Akiva – enters the orchard and returns unharmed. The other three encounter trials in the orchard which they are unable to overcome. Instead of looking at these individuals as four distinct categories of human beings, I suggest looking at them as four kinds of psychological reactions to difficult life situations where judgment becomes impaired. I wish to show how this story can offer a solution to a crisis, and how we can adopt one or all of these reactions in challenging circumstances, using each of them at different times and under various conditions.

Aḥer represents one type of rational reaction to the demands of the social world in which the individual lives. (As we shall see, R. Akiva represents a second.) He applies a rigid, fundamentalist *peshat* interpretation to reality. For instance, when he sees righteous people who die prematurely and wicked people who enjoy long, happy lives, he asks: "Is this how people who lead a Torah way of life are rewarded?" (Jerusalem Talmud, Ḥagiga 2:1). Unable to come to terms with this apparent injustice, he abandons the Torah; he is depicted as metaphorically trimming the bushes that form a fence around a field. In view of these apparent contradictions, Elisha b. Avuya sees no alternative but to emerge from the orchard as an alienated, apostate Jew – he becomes Aḥer, an Other.

The Talmud recounts that Aḥer "overhears what is said behind the curtain (that is, in heaven)" (Ḥagiga 15a): that the path to repentance is forever barred to him. He imagines God, the symbol of social justice, as having judged him and issued the verdict that the road to penitence will remain permanently closed to him. Powerless before the societal anomalies he witnessed, he abandons his society, and even accuses it of rejecting him. He sees both life and society in binary terms – the kind of perspective that young people tend to have, where everything is either black or white, where it is "I or Thou," where there is a sharp distinction between truth and falsehood. Aḥer cannot live with the inconsistencies he perceives and therefore removes himself from the norms of his society.

Ben Zoma and Ben Azzai do not grapple with a rational contradiction. Instead, they contend with the contradiction between the rational, real world, and the world of the mystical *sod*. These two figures represent two different ways of dealing with this contradiction. According to the Talmud, Ben Zoma "took one look and was injured"; in other words, he experienced a psychotic reaction. After relating the story of the orchard, the Talmud provides us with another anecdote about Ben Zoma's typical behavior after the orchard experience that helps us understand the nature of his psychotic crisis:

R. Yehoshua b. Ḥanania was standing on a small hill on the Temple Mount when he saw Ben Zoma, who did not get

up from where he was sitting [in a gesture of respect for
R. Yehoshua]. R. Yehoshua said to him, "Where have you
been, Ben Zoma, and where are you going?" Ben Zoma
replied: "I have discerned that only the span of three fin-
gers separates the water that is in heaven and the water
that is down below on earth, as it is written: 'and the spirit
of God hovered over the face of the waters' (Genesis 1:2),
like a dove that hovers above her young without touching
them." R. Yehoshua told his students: "Ben Zoma is still
outside." (Ḥagiga 15a)

Ben Zoma's situation, like Aḥer's, is depicted as an
abandonment of society. The above story opens with Ben Zoma
failing to show proper respect for his teacher: he does not rise
in his presence. The story concludes with R. Yehoshua's declaration that "Ben Zoma is still outside." However, the similarity
between Aḥer's case and that of Ben Zoma ends here. Although
Ben Zoma and Aḥer both abandon their society, they do so in
different ways: Aḥer rebels, while Ben Zoma becomes psychotic. When he sees that his student does not rise to his feet
out of deference to his mentor, R. Yehoshua asks a question
that is intended to clarify the situation, "Where have you been,
Ben Zoma, and where are you going?" Rather than judging him
hastily, R. Yehoshua tries to understand Ben Zoma's current
situation and asks how he is feeling. Ben Zoma is the typical
psychotic: he is cut off from reality, and knows neither where
he has been, nor where he is going.

Instead of providing a simple answer to R. Yehoshua's
equally simple, reality-oriented question, Ben Zoma chooses to
describe what he saw in the heavenly world. According to another
midrashic account of the story, the tension surrounding the question is intensified when R. Yehoshua, who represents normative

behavior in the real world, declares, "I call on heaven and earth as witnesses that I will not move from this spot until you tell me where your feet have been."[7] R. Yehoshua is asking Ben Zoma where his feet have been – feet that should be planted firmly on earth and which symbolize the connection with the real world.

Ben Zoma's bizarre answer reflects the state in which he finds himself: suspended somewhere between the worlds of sanity and madness. By describing the chaos that preceded the Creation and arguing that the distance between heaven and earth is not as great as everyone believes, he seeks to erase the differences between the real world, represented by the earth, and the mystical world of *sod*, represented by heaven. Ben Zoma wishes to restore the world to its primordial state of chaos, and R. Yehoshua, refusing to admit such a possibility, leaves him "outside." In the second midrashic version of this tale, R. Yehoshua's response is brilliant: he relates to the very heaven and earth that Ben Zoma refers to and calls upon them to serve as witnesses, in order to reinforce his demand that Ben Zoma return and plant his feet firmly on the earthly world.

The psychosis from which Ben Zoma suffers is rooted in his failure to distinguish between heaven and earth. He wishes to return to the symbiotic connection between a mother and her child, symbolized by the dove that hovers over her young, almost – but not quite – touching them with her wings. Swept up by this "oceanic feeling," Ben Zoma refuses to accept the distinction between the real and mystical worlds as two separate entities and thus fails to function in the real world, where respect must be shown to figures of authority (in this story, by the provision of a reality-oriented answer to a reality-oriented question).

---

7. Genesis Rabba, 2:4.

Ben Zoma's failure does not lie in his connection to the mystical world; the mystical language he uses is familiar to talmudic scholars, and even to contemporary readers. Rather, his failure lies in his inability to function simultaneously in the real and mystical worlds and to juxtapose them without one denying the existence of the other.

Ben Azzai's death appears to be the case of someone who becomes one with God (*unio mystica*) and is totally, ecstatically sucked into the vortex of the world of *sod* that lies just beyond the borders of the real world. The above talmudic tale is a tale about death, about a literal departure from this world. Let us examine another possibility – that of an ecstatic ritual in which people can appear to be exiting from the world, when they are in fact strengthening their connection to reality.

We have seen that God's act of Tzimtzum is one in which He, in a way, diminished Himself. Tzimtzum enables God to create, and allows the world to be created. Mortals may imitate this process through an ecstatic experience: we reduce or contract ourselves, to an extent negate ourselves, in order to become one with God. Nevertheless, this act of Tzimtzum enables us to create, to introduce new elements to our lives. The Banishment from the Garden of Eden, which reduced the human lifespan to 120 years, is also an incentive that spurs us to create within the limited amount of time at our disposal.

The ecstatic experience is nonetheless a dangerous one, because it can end in actual, physical death, as in the case of Ben Azzai. It is possible to include in the category of ecstatic states of consciousness a variety of mystical experiences that cause us to "exit" from ourselves, to move from the real to the mystical worlds. In different religions, this direction is depicted as unidirectional, as a journey from which no one ever returns, because it is based on a negation of the real world. Other depictions of ecstasy may help us create a fruitful dialogue between the mystical and real worlds, in which the two stand side by side, allowing us to run to and fro (like the creatures in Ezekiel's prophetic vision referred to in chapter three) along the bridge linking them. In this movement of running back and forth, the coexistence of these two worlds does not threaten us, nor does it require us to make one world come alive at the expense of the other.

In a state of *devekut*, we diminish ourselves before God and contract ourselves. Just as divine Tzimtzum makes the creation of the world possible because God is only contracting – but not eliminating – Himself, human Tzimtzum (that is not a total erasure of the ego) allows us to create. Tzimtzum can promote a relationship between the mystical and real worlds. Thus, Ben Azzai's death in a state of ecstasy may be the *Tikkun* for Ben Zoma's psychosis. Since Ben Zoma is in a state in which he cannot distinguish between the real and mystical worlds, he remains "outside" as someone who is expelled from the real world. In a state of ritualistic ecstasy, we do not allow ourselves to be sucked into the vortex of the mystical world of *sod*. Instead, we control our entries into and exits from that world, by running to and fro, ingesting minute quantities of temporary death and refusing to remain captive in the "no-man's-land" that lies between the two worlds.

R. Akiva, who according to the Talmud began to study Torah at the age of forty, is also known as the founder of midrash, as one who interprets every apparently extraneous word in the Bible, as well as each adornment on the letters in Torah scrolls. In one well-known talmudic story, Moses comes to R. Akiva's *beit midrash* and cannot understand the class. Moses is distressed, but is ultimately reassured after understanding that R. Akiva is teaching "*halakha leMoshe miSinai* (a law that Moses received at Mount Sinai)" (Menaḥot 29b). This story graphically illustrates the *paradoxical* nature of the midrash, where *derash* is placed alongside *peshat* in spite of the differences between these two methods of interpretation of the biblical text. This peaceful coexistence is made possible through the abandonment of a dialectical pattern of thinking, which decrees that two contradictory interpretations must necessarily clash.

Such is the philosophy of a mature individual, like R. Akiva, who acknowledges and comes to terms with logical contradictions. That is why R. Akiva emerges from the orchard unscathed; he survives the logical contradictions that threaten Aḥer in the orchard and which cause him to abandon normative society.[8] R. Akiva and Aḥer's reactions represent two possible ways of responding to a rational, logical contradiction. Aḥer experiences a crisis, and becomes unable to function in society. R. Akiva, in contrast, exits the orchard unscathed and leads a highly creative life.

Thus, R. Akiva's reaction is a *Tikkun*, a corrective, for Aḥer – just as Ben Azzai's response is a *Tikkun* for Ben Zoma. The former teaches us to live with contradictions; the latter, to live with the fear of death.

---

8. The Babylonian Talmud in Tractate Kiddushin (39b) relates how Elisha b. Avuya (known also as Aḥer, or "the Other") became a sinner. One day he saw a young boy climb a tree at the request of his father in order to banish a mother bird from a nest before taking the eggs she was sitting on. The young boy was thus seeking to perform two commandments (*mitzvot*): showing respect for one's parents (*kibbud av va'em*) and banishing a mother bird from a nest from which one wishes to remove the eggs (*shiluaḥ haken*). However, although the Torah explicitly states that the reward for both commandments is long life, the boy fell from the tree and died. The Tanna, Elisha b. Avuya, found the contradiction between the biblical promise and the actual outcome unbearable, and as a result, turned away from Judaism.

Appendix I

Key Concepts in Tzimtzum

Baruch Kahana and Michal Fachler

Akedatic Tzimtzum (Binding of Isaac as the model for Tzimtzum) – The father's readiness to contract himself enables the son to adopt a similar approach. Instead of the Oedipal-dialectic aspiration of one generation replacing the previous one, each generation contracts itself in order to make room for the other. Isaac is a classic example of this approach, for, in his willingness to be bound and sacrificed to God, he was in effect waiving the dialectic aspiration for expansion. This willingness on the part of the son can only arise from the absolute faith that the father is truly of the Maggidic type, that is, a father who has no desire to erase his son. Because of their mutual willingness to self-contract, the tension between past and present generations is greatly diminished; both generations focus their energies on continuity instead of on a struggle for control.

Altercentrism – In contrast with the conflict between ego-centrism (an emotional state where the ego is central) and altruism (an emotional state where the ego annuls itself for the sake of others), dialogic thinking proposes the term altercentrism, where the dialogue itself is central. In dialogue, neither side advances itself at the expense of the other. "I and Thou" exist only in a mutual relationship that is constantly evolving and in which each side can achieve self-fulfillment only by investing in and revealing itself to the other.

Anti-assertiveness – Western dialectical society offers its members a variety of ways to acquire skills that can be used in their endless struggle in the social world. Among those techniques is "assertiveness training," which is designed to teach them how to survive in a world where the guiding principle is "I or Thou." In contrast, dialogical society proposes a different approach altogether: self-negation training, or anti-assertiveness training – that is, members are taught how to make room for others (without, of course, erasing themselves totally).

Ascent through descent (*yerida letzorekh aliya*) – In the context of an exegetic analysis of the past, the failures, or descents, in that past should be viewed in accordance with the principle of "ascent through descent" (*yerida letzorekh aliya*). A descent may be regarded as a distinct stage on an ascending route. This perception, which sometimes requires *paradoxical* interpretation, can help us deal with the inevitable descents that we all experience and use them to grow emotionally and spiritually. In this context, it is possible to use such an approach to treat depression. Psychiatry sees depression as a basic state of mind, and the euphoria, or mania, that sometimes accompanies it, is regarded as a denial of the depressive state. However, it is also possible to see the relationship between the sadness and the euphoria in reverse; we may regard the depression as an unavoidable stage in a journey actually leading to a more positive state of mind.

Banishment from the Garden of Eden as the first instance of Tzimtzum – The diminishing of Adam's lifespan and power after his expulsion from the Garden of Eden exposed the secret of creative Tzimtzum that is inherent in a situation where boundaries are set.

Biographical recomposition – Ideally, our lives should be a process in which we gradually reveal the hidden light in our souls by interpreting the events in our lives and the emotions we experience. When we manage to contain all its aspects harmoniously, our narrative resembles a marvelous musical composition: a harmony consisting of many different and, in some cases, contradictory components that merge and create profound meaning. If we cannot create such a harmony, and if certain elements clash with the general direction of our lives, we experience discord. In such a state of affairs, we must therefore rewrite our musical composition, engage in biographical recomposition, which also serves us in psychological therapy, where we try to reinterpret the past by "recomposing" the various elements that it contains, including painful "failures." The result will be the creation of a new, exciting melody.

Breaking of the vessels (*Shevirat HaKelim*) – The situation created when entities are not prepared to contract themselves. Each entity aspires to expand limitlessly; war between these entities is thus inevitable. The vessels are broken when the vessels are too small for the light. In other words, each entity tries to shine its light limitlessly and does not take into consideration the vessels' capacity for receiving it.

"Bridge" between *peshat* and *sod* – Our goal is always to bridge the gap between reality as it actually is and reality as it could be – or, between the *peshat* and the *sod*. The techniques of midrash (which include the various forms of *paradoxical* thinking) help us build this bridge.

Dialectical – Any system is defined as dialectical when its parts are in a state of breakage; in such a situation, there is an endless war between the entities. Under these conditions, the only way for an entity to develop is to wage war against the other entities. This struggle between the entities creates stronger, more developed entities that have all the advantages of the entities that preceded them; the new entities defeat the older ones and continue the struggle. (To use widely accepted terminology, the struggle between thesis and antithesis results in a synthesis that, in turn, replaces the now-irrelevant thesis and antithesis.)

Dialogic – A system is defined as dialogic if its entities are prepared to contract themselves and make room for one another. This situation is not attained through dialectical struggle (an "either...or" situation) but rather the readiness of the system's entities to receive from one another without trying to dominate. The mutual Tzimtzum includes the waiving of the aspiration to expand limitlessly (a "both... and" situation).

Dimming of the light (*Imum HaOr*) – The willingness of the self-contracting entity to reveal itself to another, but only in accordance with latter's capacity to receive (that is, the capacity of the latter's "vessels") – not in accordance with the former's aspirations.

Double mirror – In therapy, mutual emulation is referred to as the "double mirror": both therapist and patient constantly reflect each other, learn about one another, and influence one another.

Eiderdown blanket – One may cope with depression in the space that extends between the individual and the community that surrounds him or her. When we cover ourselves with an eiderdown blanket, the blanket absorbs the heat of our bodies and then returns the heat in order to warm us. Similarly, when we make an effort to contribute something of ourselves to the general joy of the community (sometimes even artificially, such as through a decision to sing or dance), we are able to be a part of the collective joy. In this manner, a sense of belonging to the community can reinforce an individual's private joy.

Elevation of alien thoughts – Every thought, emotion, or flight of imagination that creates any kind of impediment (collectively, these can be referred to as "alien" thoughts) consists of a spark (*nitzotz*) and a shell (*kelipa*), which we must elevate back to its source (sometimes through the construction of a midrashic bridge between *peshat* and *derash*).

Elevation of the sparks (*Haalaat Nitzotzot*) – Turning apparent evil into good. The elevation of sparks always entails a search for vessels to contain the light that has been revealed; in other words, the elevation of sparks entails Tzimtzum.

"Evil is a chair for good" – After elevating the spark that evil formerly contained, reality expands and elevates itself. In this sense, all the reality of "evil" is the basis for a *Tikkun* that improves it far beyond what it would have been without the elevation of sparks.

Thus, instead of rejecting evil, we must seek ways to elevate the spark it contains.

Expansion (*Hitpashtut*) – The aspiration of each entity to expand and increase its power without any limitations.

Free will – Free will can be viewed as authorization from God for us to act freely and to make our own decisions, although He knows in advance what those decisions will be. We all have the ability at any time to decide whether we want to relate to reality in a dialogic manner or to remain in a dialectic mindset.

Greatness and smallness, running to and fro (*ratzo vashov*) – Our lives have moments of greatness, spiritual elevation, joy, and clear-headed thinking; however, they cannot be filled solely with such moments. There must also be moments of smallness, which have a unique importance in themselves, because, at such times, we sink deep within ourselves in order to connect with the simple, material side of life. Our lives are a constant oscillation between the two poles of greatness and smallness and are filled with a continual "running to and fro" (*ratzo vashov*). Dialogical thinking assigns legitimacy to both states, regarding each of them as containing a special spark and considering the ideal situation to be one of constant, free movement between these two poles.

Haatzala **(Inspiration)** – God's transfer of part of His spirit to the world. *Haatzala* depicts the Creation as occurring within God Himself.

Ḥutzpa – In a dialogic intergenerational relationship, the new generation, although still subject to the control of the previous one, is encouraged to express itself freely, even to the point of audacity (*ḥutzpa*), the working assumption being that the new generation is not rebelling simply for the sake of rebelling, but is instead expressing the inner spark of youth.

"I and Thou" (instead of "I or Thou") – In interpersonal relations, the conflict between the dialectical and dialogic approaches is expressed in the conflict between the "I and Thou" approach (where I and Thou are members of a single system and each receives meaning from their interrelationship) and the "I or Thou" approach (where there is a struggle in which one of the entities aims to defeat the other).

"In all thy ways acknowledge Him" (Prov. 3:6) – Commerce and Torah study are not the sole activities in any social system. We can all reveal our inner light and shape our unique path in this world. There is no one ideal path nor is any path essentially forbidden; all paths lead to the revelation of our unique inner light of our souls. If a certain path is destructive in its consequences, there is a need for elevating sparks in order to reveal the hidden light it contains.

Inclusive diagnosis – Within the context of the double mirror concept, one can point to an alternative approach to psychiatric diagnosis. In contrast with the psychiatric concept of the differentiating diagnosis, which is intended to emphasize the distinction between the "patient" or "deviant" and the "sane" individual who suits the accepted social ideal, inclusive diagnosis emphasizes the similarities between the patient and apparently "sane" people.

Inner light (*Reshimu*) – The impression that remains after the vessels have been broken. This is the reduced light that reveals itself to the receiving entity after having been adjusted to the capacity of the entity's receiving vessels.

Issachar-Zebulun relationship – Dialogical thought also pertains to the relationship between various strata in the population. In Jewish tradition, Issachar is perceived as the Torah scholar, the spiritual and intellectual individual, whereas Zebulun is seen as the merchant, the practical individual (in hasidic terms: the individual representing form versus the individual representing matter). In the dialogic world, instead of class war (which, in the Middle Ages, was a war between Church and Empire), there is an alternative relationship – one that is characterized by mutual Tzimtzum, namely, the Issachar-Zebulun relationship. Additionally, the dynamics of the Issachar-Zebulun relationship, founded on love, respect, and mutual give-and-take, and which brings together two individuals so radically different from one another, constitutes a classic example of an altercentric relationship.

Karaism – According to this approach, there is only one way of interpreting a text – a literal interpretation. If we transpose this kind of thinking to psychology, Karaism dictates that there is only one true narrative and that all we must do is to reveal it (this was psychoanalysis's approach in its initial phase). The Karaite approach is dialectical and creates a constant struggle between the various understandings of a text's "literal interpretation."

Legend and myth – The difference between legend and myth lies in the fact that legend is created from realistic elements. Myth, on the other hand, blends wondrous supernatural events and thus breaks with familiar natural reality. Thus, whereas legend may be categorized under the rubric of *derash*, myth can be classified as *sod.* It is possible, sometimes even necessary, to stretch a dialogic bridge between the rational, realistic content of legend, and the superrational content of myth.

Legend and narrative – Each of us has a unique life story that can be called a narrative, which characterizes an individual's subjective experience. However, the narrative does not exist in a vacuum; there is a dialogical relationship between the story that we tell about ourselves (our narrative) and the story that others tell about us in our immediate social setting (life legend). Both our narrative and life legend are essential for a proper understanding of our life story, and it is impossible to understand the narrative without the legend; the same is true in reverse. This is the difference between the Jewish view and the postmodern perception, where each person has a narrative that is not necessarily connected to his or her social legend.

Letter rearrangement – One method of reading a text is to rearrange the letters of some of its key words in order to uncover hidden meanings. The Hebrew language supplies a wealth of opportunities for such letter rearrangements. For instance, the letters *nun-gimel-ayin* of *nega*, blow, punishment, or affliction, can be rearranged as *ayin-nun-gimel* to read *oneg*, pleasure. Similarly, the letters *tav-yod-nun-vav-kuf* of *tinok*, infant, can be rearranged as *tav-yod-kuf-vav-nun* to read *tikkun*, correction.

Light – Every entity yearns to reveal itself to another; "light" is the term used to describe this aspiration. Hasidism's basic assumption is that light is always good and the desire to reveal it stems from the wish to provide benefit. All people have their own unique light and their profoundest aspiration is to uncover it.

Maggidic father – The dialogue on *Tikkun* begins in the relationship between generations. In contrast with Laius (Oedipus' dialectical father, who feared that his son would usurp him), we have the parable of the Maggid of Mezeritch about the father who is prepared to contract himself in order to allow his son to find a place for himself in the world.

***Mikdash* and midrash** – In contrast with Karaism, Jewish thinking is built on a continual dialogic give-and-take between a fixed, unchanging element, which can be called *mikdash* (temple), and a pluralistic one that is open to an infinite number of interpretations, termed midrash. A fascinating example of this dialogic tension is biblical exegesis, which is based on a biblical text that cannot be altered even in the slightest manner, and the infinite number of different, sometimes even contradictory, interpretations that are offered for that text.

Multi-labeling versus mono-labeling – A dialectical society tends to propose one path by which its members can earn social esteem and a solid social standing. In a dialectical society, some people are pushed into the margins or are defined as "deviants." In contrast, a dialogical society follows the principle of "In all thy ways acknowledge Him" and regards a very wide range of paths as ideal, thereby accepting all its members. Thus, in a dialogical society, there is the concept of multi-labeling; dialectical society, where there is only one dominant label that is the "proper path," is characterized by mono-labeling.

Mutual emulation – Western psychology has created philosophies of unilateral emulation, where individuals develop by emulating role models such as parents, teachers, and culture heroes, and where the role models themselves are not influenced by the individuals emulating them. In contrast, the altercentric approach of "I and Thou" sees both sides as participating in an interactive relationship, where they influence and reflect one another. Only by agreeing to be influenced by the other party can the stronger side in this interaction also have influence.

Mutual responsibility ("All Jews are responsible for one another") – Society is not comprised of individuals who are essentially egocentric and who build it in collaboration or competition with one another. Quite the contrary, society incorporates individuals who find the meaning of their lives in society *per se*, and who discover others and reveal themselves to others by making an altercentric contribution to the general good, to which they feel a deep sense of responsibility. This concept is expressed in an important principle in Jewish tradition: "All Jews are responsible for one another."

Paradox/paradoxical – The principal tool of the exegetic perception of the past is *paradoxical* interpretation. This form of interpretation seeks to reveal possibilities that might provide new opportunities for a biographical recomposition of a person's narrative and thereby for the revelation of new sparks that have not yet been seen in the course of that person's life. The method for attaining this goal is *paradox* – a simultaneous perception of contradictory elements in a new context that is capable of containing all of them.

PaRDeS – In Jewish thought, it is customary to perceive many different layers in any given text, none of which is contradictory. Among these layers are *peshat* (literal interpretation), *derash* (homiletical interpretation), *remez* (symbolic or allegorical interpretation), and *sod* (mystical interpretation). These four concepts constitute the PaRDes approach to reading a text. The PaRDeS approach may be used to combine different therapeutic methods perceived as contradictory in today's world of therapeutic thinking. We can deal with the realistic *peshat,* using rationalist, behavioral methods, such as cognitive and behaviorist treatment; there is also room for investigating a patient's past and for "recomposing" his or her life story; and there is also a place for an acceptance of mystical, emotional reality.

Pro-rehabilitation – In line with the concept of "ascent through descent," "rehabilitation" from descent (meaning a return to the point that preceded the descent) is inadequate. The descent must be regarded as a stage in an ascent to a point where we have never been. In other words, rehabilitation is not enough and must be combined with progress; hence, pro-rehabilitation (progress + rehabilitation). Even the deepest descent contains a spark (*nitzotz*) that we must elevate from the shell (*kelipa*) that caused the descent.

Returning sparks to their divine origin – The elevation of alien thoughts changes their appearance and our attitude toward them; however, we are not arbitrarily distorting them but are actually exposing the spark that they initially contained. In this manner, we are returning the sparks in these alien thoughts to their source.

Self-negation versus prominence – Whereas, in a dialectical society, all members seek prominence and want to "stand out," in a dialogical society, its members can negate themselves (but not totally) *vis-à-vis* others. The self-negation in a dialogical society is actually a waiving of the desire to be prominent in an exaggerated manner (that is, to expand limitlessly) and represents an overall readiness on the part of its members for mutual Tzimtzum.

Shivim panim laTorah (the Torah can be interpreted in seventy ways) – In dialogue, no interpretation is totally rejected; even a blatantly destructive interpretation has some elements of light and its sparks must be elevated. From its very beginnings, as seen in classic rabbinical sources, Jewish thinking has always demonstrated how this principle can be applied to the reading of texts, in accordance with the dictum, *shivim panim laTorah* ("the Torah can be interpreted in seventy [that is, an infinite number of] ways"). Contemporary psychology may also adopt this principle to help patients. In the context of psychology, this principle means that none of us has only one narrative; we all have several, parallel narratives, each of which represents one aspect of our lives or one particular "spark" that is aspiring to express itself. We are all deeper and richer (spiritually) than any narrative that we choose to create. It is important to emphasize, however, that not every narrative is acceptable. There may be narratives that are mistaken or destructive but, nonetheless, contain a spark of light and which do have a place in our lives.

Sparks and shells (*nitzotzot* and *kelipot*) – In every possible reality, two components can be discerned: the good light that aspires to expand and the destructiveness that is the basic element of apparent evil. In kabbalistic language, these components are called sparks and shells respectively.

Tikkun (correction) – A corrected situation is when each entity agrees to limit its light and to take into consideration both the existence and receptive capacity of another entity. In a *Tikkun* where the light is great and the vessels small, the light is diminished and efforts are directed toward the construction of vessels capable of receiving that light.

Tzimtzum – An entity's willingness to contract itself in order to make room for others. (Obviously, in Tzimtzum, an entity is waiving to a certain extent its desire to expand; however, it is not a total waiving of this desire. The self-contracting entity does not erase itself but simply makes room for others in order to reveal itself to them.)

Vessels (*Kelim*) – Each entity has vessels uniquely suited for receiving light, such as its ability to recognize light and its ability to contain emotions. When these vessels receive a quantity of light that they are capable of containing, they develop and their ability to contain light steadily increases.

Yetzer/yetzira (**urge/creativity**) – The connection between the empirical reality of the *peshat* and the mystical reality of the *sod* also appears in the relationship between the world of urges (especially the sexual urge) and spiritual creativity. Whereas blatantly mystical elements of ecstasy appear in the sexual urge, erotic elements of desire appear in spiritual creativity. In dialogical thinking, urges and creativity are in a relationship of mutual dialogical Tzimtzum, in which there is room for both the sexual urge and spiritual creativity as two unique aspects of the human soul and human vitality, without any need arising to choose one of these two as a Karaite fundamentalist "truth."

Appendix II

Basic Assumptions and Questions of Therapy

BASIC ASSUMPTIONS

What should I assume when I meet someone?

- He has a life story, which reveals his singular qualities (his light, soul, holy spark) within the unique toolbox he has inherited (here we refer to the influence of various factors, including social setting, on this individual).
- He is interested in revealing to me some of his unique light.
- His distress stems from the fact that his inner light is encountering difficulty revealing itself in reality (the problem of *kelipot*).
- His light can reveal itself in an optimal manner through a dialogical system that includes the "I and Thou" in a situation of mutual Tzimtzum.

- His distress is connected to the existence of a dialectical situation of "I or Thou." In such a situation, certain qualities or inner voices cannot reveal themselves. In the terminology of Tzimtzum we would say that, in this situation, one entity is seeking to expand or dominate and that, only through the Tzimtzum of those elements can the other elements reveal themselves.
- If we can overcome the *kelipot*, a new light that has never revealed itself before will do so. (Here we are referring to pro-rehabilitation, not to rehabilitation, in the sense of "evil is a chair for good.")
- The best way to help him overcome his distress is to restructure his life story so that his inner light can reveal itself (biographical recomposition). This can be done through a midrashic creation that we help designing; in this creation, his life story will be told in a manner that can provide both a *Tikkun* of the past and hope for the future.

KEY QUESTIONS

Questions I should ask myself in a treatment encounter:

- What are the special qualities of the individual whom I am now encountering (the patient, if this is a treatment situation)?
- Which qualities are unable to express themselves in the life of the individual I am now encountering?
- What is preventing them from expressing themselves (or, what are the dialectical *kelipot* that are preventing these qualities from revealing themselves)?
- Are there similar *kelipot* inside me? (Here is the place for the all-inclusive diagnosis and for the double mirror of mutual emulation.)

- Which element is overly dominant and must be contracted (or must contract itself) so that the other elements can reveal themselves?
- How can I establish a dialogue with the patient in order to create an inner dialogue inside him, so that his inner voices can reveal themselves and so that his negative inner voices (that is, the dialectical *kelipot*) can be contracted (or can contract themselves)?
- In which other ways can the patient's autobiography be told (so that he can participate in the "biographical recomposition" of his life story) and which of these ways can provide him with a feeling of hope and meaning?

Bibliography

SECONDARY HEBREW SOURCES

Aboulafia, M. *HaGanan VeHaPri: HaMadrikh HaKatan LeHayim Me'usharim.* Jerusalem, 5769 (2008–2009).

Agnon, S.Y. *Sippurim VaAggadot.* Tel Aviv, 1959.

Ashlag, Y.L. *Mavo LeSefer HaZohar.* In: Ashlag, Y.L., *Sefer HaZohar Im Peirush HaSulam.* Jerusalem, 5715 (1954–1955). Pp. xxvii–xxviii.

Baal Shem Tov (Besht), I. *Keter Shem Tov.* Jerusalem, 1975.

————. *Sefer HaBesht Al HaTorah.* Jerusalem, 1975.

————. *Tzavaat HaRivash.* New York, 1975.

Beer, M. "Issachar and Zebulun." In: *Bar-Ilan Yearbook.* Ramat-Gan, 1968.

Bergman, S.H. *HaFilosofia HaDialogit Mi-Kierkegaard ad Buber.* Jerusalem, 1974.

Buber, M. *BeSod Siah: Al Adam VaAmidato Nokhah HaHavaya.* Jerusalem, 5724 (1963–1964).

————. *Netivot BeUtopia.* Tel Aviv, 1983.

_____. *Or HaGanuz: Sippurei Ḥasidim*. Tel Aviv, 1976.

Dov Baer, Maggid of Mezeritch. *Maggid Devarav LeYaakov*. Lublin, 1927.

Dubnow, S. *Toldot HaḤasidut*. Tel Aviv, 1975.

Foucault, M. *Toldot HaShiga'on BeIdan HaTevuna*. Trans. Aharon Amir. Jerusalem, 1986.

Freud, S. *Moshe HaIsh VeEmunat HaYiḥud* [*Moses and Monotheism*]. Translation and afterword by Moshe Atar. Tel Aviv, 5739 (1978–1979).

Garb, Y. *Yeḥidei HaSegulot Yehiyu LaAdarim: Iyunim BeKabbalat HaMe'a HaEsrim*. Jerusalem, 2005.

Hegel, G.W.F. *Hakdama LaFenomonologia Shel HaRuaḥ*. Translated and explained by Yirmiyahu Yovel. Jerusalem, 5756 (1995–1996).

Horodetsky, S.A., ed. *Sefer Shivḥei HaBaal Shem Tov*. Tel Aviv, 5735 (1974–1975).

Jacob Joseph of Polonne. *Toldot Yaakov Yosef*. Jerusalem, 1963.

Kahane, B. *The Breaking [of the Vessels] and Their Repair as a Paradigm for Psychopathology and Psychotherapy*. PhD Dissertation. Jerusalem, 5765 (2004–2005).

Kariv, A. *Kitvei Maharal MiPrag*. Jerusalem, 5720 (1959–1960).

Lederberg, N. *Sod HaDaat: Demuto HaRuḥanit VeHanhagato HaHevratit Shel Rabbi Yisrael Baal Shem Tov*. Jerusalem, 5767 (2006–2007).

Maimon, S. *Ḥayei Shlomo Maimon (Katuv Bidei Atzmo)*. Trans. Y.L. Baruch. Tel Aviv, 5702 (1941–1942).

Mauss, M. *Al HaMatana*. Trans. Hila Karas. Tel Aviv, 2005.

Nachman of Bratslav. *Ḥayei Moharan*. Jerusalem, 1952.

_____. *Likutei Moharan*. Jerusalem, 5740 (1979–1980).

Nietzsche, F. *Maavar LeTov ULeRa: LeGene'alogia Shel HaMussar* [*On the Genealogy of Morals*]. Trans. Israel Eldad. Tel Aviv, 5728 (1967–1968).

Nigal, G., ed. *Torot Baal HaToladot: Derashot Rabbi Yaakov Yosef MiPolonne, Lefi Nosei Yesod.* Jerusalem, 5734 (1973–1974).

Piekarz, M. *Bimei Tzemihat HaHasidut.* Jerusalem, 1978.

Plato. *Plato's Writings [Kitvei Aplaton].* Trans. Yehuda G. Liebes. Jerusalem and Tel Aviv, 5735 (1974–1975).

Rotenberg, M. *Al HaHayim VeHaAlmavet, Dimuyei Gan Eden KeMe'atzvei Hitnahagut: Natzrut, Islam, Yahadut.* Jerusalem, 5768 (2007–2008).

_____. *Between Rationality and Irrationality.* New Brunswick, 2004.

_____. *Creativity and Sexuality.* New Brunswick, 2005.

_____. *HaHayim KeMassa Tanakhi.* Jerusalem, 2012.

_____. *Hasidic Psychology.* New Brunswick, 2004.

_____. *Natzrut UPsikhiatria: HaTeologia SheMeAhorei HaPsikhologia.* Israel, 5755 (1994–1995).

_____. *Psikhologia Yehudit VeHasidut: HaPsikhologia SheMeAhorei HaTeologia.* Israel, 1997 (second ed.).

_____. *Shekhol VeHaAggada HaHaya: Lo HaMaaseh Ikar Ella HaMaasiya.* Tel Aviv, 2005.

_____. *Rewriting the Self.* New Brunswick, 2004.

Schatz-Uffenheimer, R. *HaHasidut KeMistika: Yesodot Kviyetistiim BaMahshava HaHasidit BaMe'a HaShmoneh Esrei.* Jerusalem, 5728 (1967–1968).

Scholem, G. *Devarim BeEgo.* Tel Aviv, 1976.

Schwartzman, O. *Rofeh Lavan, Eilim Shehorim: Refuat Nefesh Maaravit BaJungel Shel Afrika.* Tel Aviv, 5767 (2006–2007).

Shatil, J. *Kontzeptziyot HaEnergia HaNafshit BeTorot Ishiyot Psikhologiyot UVaTefisa HaKabbalit-Hasidit: Darkhei Mimusha BiYshivat Baalei Teshuva Shel Hasidei Bratslav.* PhD Dissertation. Jerusalem, 1987.

Steinman, E. *Kitvei Rabbi Nachman MiBratslav.* Tel Aviv, 1951.

_____. *Shaar HaHasidut.* Tel Aviv, 1957.

Suzuki, D.T. *Mavo LeZen Buddhism*. Trans. Saul Shiloh. Hod Hasharon, 1999.

Tishby, I. *Torat HaRa VeHaKlipa BeKabbalat HaAri*. Jerusalem, 5720 (1959–1960).

Weber, M. *HaEtika HaProtestantit VeRuah HaKapitalism*. Trans. Baruch Moran. Tel Aviv, 5744 (1983–1984).

Weiss, J., "The Beginnings of Hasidism." In: Rubinstein, A., ed., *Perakim BeTorat HaHasidut UVeToldoteha*. Jerusalem, 5738 (1977–1978). Pp. 46–105.

OTHER SECONDARY SOURCES

Alberti, R.E. and Emmons, M.L. *Stand Up, Speak Out, Talk Back!* New York, 1977.

Angyal, A. *Neurosis and Treatment: A Holistic Approach*. New York, 1965.

Bakan, D. *The Duality of Human Existence*. Boston, 1966.

Bandura, A. *Principles of Behavior Modification*. New York, 1969.

Bauer, B. *Die Judenfrage*. Baraschweig, 1843.

Bebbington, P.E. "The Epidemiology of Depressive Disorders." *Culture, Medicine and Psychiatry* 2 (1978): 297–341.

Beck, A.T. *Depression*. Philadelphia, 1975.

————. *Cognitive Therapy and Emotional Disorders*. New York, 1979.

Bellah, R.N. *Tokugava Religion*. Boston, 1970.

Berger, P. *Invitation to Sociology*. New York, 1963.

Bettelheim, B. *The Uses of Enchantment*. New York, 1977.

Boisen, A.T. "The Genesis and Significance of Mystical Identification in Cases of Mental Disorder." *Psychiatry* 15 (1952): 287–296.

Boorstin, D.J. *Democracy and Its Discontents*. New York, 1974.

Browne, H. *How I Found Freedom in an Unfree World*. New York, 1974.

Buber, M. *Hasidism and the Modern Man*. New York, 1958.

_____. *Between Man and Man.* New York, 1967.

Calvin, J.A. *Compend of the Institutes of the Christian Religion.* Philadelphia, 1939.

Campbell, J. *Myths to Live by.* New York, 1978.

Cohen, A.K. *Delinquent Boys.* New York, 1955.

Doi, T. *The Anatomy of Dependence.* Tokyo, 1969.

Dresner, S.H. *The Zaddik.* New York, 1960.

Durkheim, E. *The Division of Labor in Society.* New York, 1964.

Eisenstadt, S.N. *Max Weber on Charisma and Institution-Building.* Chicago, 1968.

Eliade, M. *Shamanism: Archaic Techniques of Ecstasy.* London, 1964.

_____. *The Myth of the Eternal Return.* Princeton, 1974.

Fensterheim, H. and Baer, J. *Don't Say Yes When You Want to Say No.* New York, 1975.

Fingarette, H. *The Self in Transformation.* New York, 1963.

Foucault, M. *The History of Sexuality: An Introduction.* New York, 1990.

Frankl, V.E. *The Doctor and the Soul.* Middlesex, 1965.

Freud, S. *Complete Psychological Works.* Vol. 4. London, 1900.

_____. *The Basic Writings of Sigmund Freud.* New York, 1938.

Friedman, M.S. *Martin Buber: The Life of Dialogue.* New York, 1971.

Fromm, E. *The Fear from Freedom.* London, 1960.

Gouldner, A.W. "The Norms of Reciprocity." In: Biddle, B.J. and Thomas, E.J., eds., *Role Theory: Concepts and Research.* New York, 1966.

Haring, D., ed. *Personal Character and Cultural Milieu.* New York, 1956.

Hegel, G.W. *Philosophy of History.* New York, 1900.

Heifetz, H. *Zen and Hasidism.* London, 1978.

Idel, M. "Universalization and Integration: Two Conceptions of Mystical Union in Jewish Mysticism." In: Idel, M. and McGinn, B., eds., *Mystical Union and Monotheistic Faith: An Ecumenical Dialogue.* New York, 1996. Pp. 27–57.

Jacobs, L. *Hasidic Prayer*. New York, 1978.

Johnson, C.L. and Johnson, F.A. "Interaction Rules and Ethnicity." *Social Forces* 54 (1973): 452–466.

Kaiser, W. *Praisers of Folly*. Cambridge, 1963.

Kant, I. *Religion within the Limits of Reason Alone*. New York, 1960.

Kiev, A. *Transcultural Psychiatry*. New York, 1972.

Klostermaier, K. *Liberation, Salvation, Self-Realization*. Madras, 1973.

Kraepelin, E. *Psychiatrie*. Leipzig and Bristol, 1909.

Laing, R.D. *The Divided Self*. Middlesex, 1965.

_____. *The Politics of Experience*. New York, 1967.

Lasch, C. *The Culture of Narcissism*. New York, 1979.

Leavy, S.A. *The Psychoanalytic Dialogue*. New Haven, 1980.

Löwith, K. *Meaning in History: The Theological Implications of the Philosophy of History*. Chicago, 1957.

Malinowski, B. *Argonauts of the Western Pacific*. New York, 1961.

McMullin, R.E. *Handbook of Cognitive Therapy Techniques*. New York, 1986.

Mead, G.H. *Mind, Self and Society*. Chicago, 1934.

Merton, R.K. *Social Theory and Social Structure*. New York, 1958.

Mussen, G.P. "Early Socialization: Learning and Identification." In: G. Mandler et al., eds., *New Directions in Psychology III*. New York, 1967.

Nakane, C. *Japanese Society*. Berkeley, 1970.

Nisbet, R.A. *Social Change and History*. New York, 1979.

Nordland, O. "Shamanism and the 'Unreal.'" In: Edsman, C.M., ed., *Studies in Shamanism*. Stockholm, 1967.

Nottingham, E. *Religion: A Sociological View*. New York, 1971.

Page, J.D. *Psychopathology*. New York, 1971.

Pelletier, K.R. and Garfield, C. *Consciousness East and West*. New York, 1976.

Perls, F.S. *Gestalt Therapy Verbatim*. Lafayette, 1969.

Poll, S. *The Hasidic Community in Williamsburg*. New York, 1973.

Rabinowicz, H.M. *The World of Hasidism*. London, 1970.

Rieff, P. *Freud: The Mind of the Moralist*. New York, 1961.

Rotenberg, M. "Conceptual and Methodological Notes on Affective and Cognitive Role-Taking (Sympathy and Empathy): An Illustrative Experiment with Delinquent and Non-Delinquent Boys." *Journal of Genetic Psychology* 125 (1974): 177–185.

_____. *Damnation and Deviance: The Protestant Ethic and the Spirit of Failure*. New York, 1978.

_____. *Re-Biographing and Deviance*. New York, 1987.

Sarbin, T.R. "The Concept of Hallucination." *Journal of Personality* 35 (1967): 359–380.

_____. "Schizophrenic Thinking: A Role Theoretical Analysis." *Journal of Personality* 37 (1969): 190–209.

Sarbin, T.R. and Adler, N. "Self-Reconstruction Processes: A Preliminary Report." *The Psychoanalytic Review* 57 (1970–1971): 599–616.

Schafer, R. *The Analytic Attitude*. New York, 1983.

Schatzman, M. *Soul Murder: Persecution in the Family*. New American Library, 1976.

Scholem, G. *Major Trends in Jewish Mysticism*. New York, 1941.

_____. *The Messianic Idea in Judaism*. New York, 1972.

_____. Opening Address. In: Werblowsky, R.J.Z. and Bleeker, C.J., eds., *Types of Redemption*. Jerusalem, 1968.

Segal, S.P. and Aviram, U. *The Mentally Ill in Community-Based Sheltered Care*. New York, 1978.

Sennett, E.R. *The Fall of Public Man*. New York, 1977.

Sennett, E.R. and Sachson, A.D., eds. *Transitional Facilities in the Rehabilitation of the Emotionally Disturbed*. Manhattan, 1970.

Shelef, L. *Generations Apart*. New York, 1981.

Sica, A. *Weber, Irrationality and Social Order*. Berkeley, 1988.

Silverman, J. "Shamans and Acute Schizophrenia." *American Anthropologist* 69 (1967): 21–31.

Spense, D.E. *Narrative Truth and Historical Truth.* New York, 1982.

Suzuki, D.T. *Mysticism, Christian and Buddhist.* New York, 1971.

Teshima, J.Y. "Self-Extinction in Zen and Hasidism." In: Heifetz, H., ed., *Zen and Hasidism.* London, 1978. Pp. 108–117.

Toynbee, A. *A Study of History.* London, 1934.

Tucker, R. *Philosophy and Myth in Karl Marx.* Cambridge, 1967.

Ullman, L.D. and Krasner, L. *A Psychological Approach to Abnormal Behavior.* New York, 1969.

Veblen, T. *The Theory of the Leisure Class.* New York, 1934.

Warren, R. *The Community in America.* Chicago, 1963.

Watts, A. *Psychotherapy East and West.* New York, 1975.

Weber, M. *The Sociology of Religion.* Boston, 1967.

Weeks, G.R. "Towards a Dialectical Approach to Intervention." *Human Development* 20 (1977): 277–292.

Zax, M. and Cowen, E.L. *Abnormal Psychology.* New York, 1972.

Zilboorg, A.G. *A History of Medical Psychology.* New York, 1941.

About the Rotenberg Center
for Jewish Psychology

The Rotenberg Center for Jewish Psychology was founded for the purpose of advancing Jewish psychology as a powerful therapeutic tool and as a comprehensive communal and educational perception of society.

For over thirty years, Israel Prize laureate and Hebrew University of Jerusalem Professor Mordechai Rotenberg has conducted research in his fields of scholarly expertise and has published twelve books and countless articles, creating a consistent, coherent theory of Jewish psychology. Judaism and its monotheistic ethics have had a far-reaching impact on the Western world. By presenting the thinking of Professor Rotenberg as part of Judaism's diverse culture, Jewish psychology has been elevated to the center of the arena of public discourse shaping Jewish identity. The language of Western psychology is anchored in egocentric and individualistic perceptions that emphasize the self and have

spread throughout Western society. The influence of those perceptions on Western society expresses itself in various ways: feelings
of loneliness and alienation, relationships prominently expressing
rivalry, and power struggles.

Professor Rotenberg's work offers an alternative approach
that can bring about a radical change in Western society's psychological language – in both the professional and the popular
versions – and which may contribute to the healing of these social
symptoms. Basing himself on the Jewish tradition of mutual
responsibility ("All Jews are responsible for one another") and
on the talmudic method of *shivim panim laTorah* ("the Torah can
be interpreted in seventy [that is, an infinite number of] ways"),
Professor Rotenberg has identified psychological principles that
can be found "between the lines" in classical rabbinic literature,
in midrashim, in Kabbala, and primarily in hasidic thought. Using
these principles as his infrastructure, he has formulated a psychological paradigm of the notion of Tzimtzum. The model is based
on the idea of divine Tzimtzum: by contracting Himself, God
makes room for Creation and His creatures. This concept is a
psychological and sociological model that has implications for
our interpersonal relationships.

Training programs, seminars, one-day conferences, and
publications are some of the tools through which the Rotenberg
Center for Jewish Psychology advances the theory of Jewish
psychology that Professor Rotenberg has developed. A two-year
course for professionals in the social sciences (social workers,
psychologists, and educational advisers) is offered by the Center.
Participants in this course acquire the theoretical background and
practical tools that they can use in applying Jewish psychology in
their professional work. In addition, the Center hosts an annual
study evening for the public that presents different aspects of
Jewish psychology.

About the Rotenberg Center for Jewish Psychology

The Rotenberg Center for Jewish Psychology was founded in 2006 to commemorate the memory of Boaz Israel Rotenberg, the youngest son of Professor Rotenberg and his wife Naomi, who fell in combat in the course of his military service in the Israel Defense Forces.

For further information on the programs of the Rotenberg Center for Jewish Psychology, you can visit the Center's website: www.jewishpsychology.org.il

The fonts used in this book are from the Arno family

Maggid Books
The best of contemporary Jewish thought from
Koren Publishers Jerusalem Ltd.